The Action Learner's Toolkit

The
Action Learner's
Toolkit

John Edmonstone

GOWER

Published by
Gower Publishing Limited
Gower House
Croft Road
Aldershot
Hampshire GU11 3HR
England

Gower
Suite 420
101 Cherry Street
Burlington VT 05401-4405 USA

British Library Cataloguing in Publication Data
Edmonstone, John
    The action learner's toolkit
    1. Employees – Training of 2. Active learning
    I. Title
    658.3'124'04

Library of Congress Cataloging-in-Publication Data
Edmonstone, John.
    The action learner's toolkit / John Edmonstone.
      p. cm.
    Includes bibliographical references (p. 83).
    ISBN 0-566-08466-X (alk. paper)
      1. Active learning--Handbooks, manuals, etc. I. Title.

LB1027.23.E36 2003
371.39--dc21

2002027161

ISBN 0566 08466 X

Typeset in Plantin Light by IML Typographers, Birkenhead, Merseyside and printed in England by MPG Books Ltd., Bodmin, Cornwall.

Contents

List of figures and tables

FIGURES

Tables

Acknowledgements

There are a number of people who deserve thanks in helping me (sometimes unwittingly!) in the production of this toolkit. Thanks are due, first, to Reg Revans who I first met in the 1970s at a learning disabilities hospital in Derbyshire while he was attempting to interest the UK National Health Service in action learning. The passion with which he communicated the simple yet powerful nature of action learning made a profound impression on someone then beginning a career in organization and management development. Second, to Mike Pedler, whom I met shortly afterwards and who has been a continuing supporter of action learning in its many manifestations when it has been both in and out of fashion. Third, to those members of learning sets which I have facilitated over the years (particularly the change agents and people working in primary health care) who have exposed me to many of the areas addressed in this toolkit.

Finally, my thanks to Carol, my own 'comrade in adversity' for enduring the birth of this toolkit and for all her support and challenge over the years.

Introduction

Reg Revans outlined the *principles* of Action Learning – but not always how to implement them. His ideas were never a package of delivery.

(Margerison, 2000)

I have three objectives in writing *The Action Learner's Toolkit*. First, I want to demystify action learning, to free it from the esoteric and make it as accessible as possible to as many people as possible.

When, as one of the co-authors of *The Facilitator's Toolkit* (Havergal and Edmonstone, 1999), I came across one disparaging review which claimed in a fairly dismissive way that the target audience was only 'managers and others who may find themselves called upon to do some workplace facilitation', rather than management and organization development specialists, I actively rejoiced, for that was just the audience we were interested in! For this reason there are relatively few mentions of managers and management in this toolkit, but many of people, on the basis that action learning has a wider application than just this group and that activity.

The target population is therefore a wide one. It includes people who might wish to consider action learning as a development approach, those who might be facilitating action learning sets and those who will be participants in such sets.

My second objective is to acknowledge and celebrate that action learning is founded on a set of coherent principles which reflect our understanding of both adult learning and organizational change. The toolkit will clarify these principles and highlight the linkages to other relevant work. Part 1 of the toolkit summarizes the key principles of action learning.

Finally (and especially in the light of Margerison's comment above), I wish to acknowledge that action learning is a flexible and adaptive approach which needs to be designed to suit the unique requirements of the people and organizations where it is adopted, but also to accept that there is now a growing body of emerging good practice which can usefully be shared to prevent the continuing reinvention of the wheel.

Part 2 of this toolkit identifies good practice under a number of headings, ranging from action learning problems and projects, through action learning set composition and working, to the evaluation of action learning, so forming a compendium of useful material.

The bibliography, at the end of the book, aims to be comprehensive and wide-ranging, including a number of organization-based case studies as well as more conceptual material.

There is, of course, a paradox here – the act of capturing and writing down such practice turns what Revans called questioning insight into programmed knowledge, but this toolkit is in no sense a prescribed rulebook. Action learning is robust enough and set members and set advisers independent-minded enough to use some of the emerging practice logged here in a thoughtful and selective manner.

A final word about the aphorisms scattered throughout the toolkit. This was a practice adopted by Reg Revans who peppered his publications with quotations from the Bible and the works of the Buddha. They are intended as pockets of light which encapsulate complex ideas in a simple yet effective phrase and hopefully illuminate some of the principles and practice of this toolkit.

Part 1

The Principles of Action Learning

Chapter 1

Defining action learning: what is it and what is it for?

The range of what we think and do is limited by what we fail to notice, and because we fail to notice that we fail to notice, there is little we can do to change, until we notice how failing to notice shapes our thoughts and deeds.

(Ronald Laing)

There are plenty of useful definitions of Action Learning (McGill and Beaty, 1992; Pedler, 1996; Raelin, 2000) but at the core of all of them is the idea that action learning is:

- a method for individual and organization development
- based upon small groups of colleagues meeting over time to tackle real problems or issues in order to get things done; reflecting and learning with and from their experience and from each other as they attempt to change things.

This may seem deceptively simple but it embodies ideas about adult learning and organizational change which are both complex and central to what action learning is about.

ADULT LEARNING

From the world of adult learning come the notions that:

- People learn only when they want to do so, and not when others want them to. In other words, effective learning is self-directed, voluntary, intentional and purposeful. It is an active, not a passive process.
- A great deal of learning is episodic rather than continuous. Learning takes place in short bursts of relatively intensive activity, absorbing the learner's attention. It usually comes to an end when the immediate purpose of learning (the resolving of a problem) has been achieved. People then resort again to a much slower pace of learning before the next such intensive episode occurs, again triggered by a problem which requires resolution.
- We feel the urge to learn when we are faced with difficulties we would like to overcome. We all face work and life problems which provide us with the motivation to learn.

- A major block to learning can be a predisposing mental set formed by previous experience. Everyone needs to realize when their mental set may no longer be valid and may need revising. People learn best when they are able to question the basic assumptions on which their actions are based. Therefore review and reassessment of all experience (knowledge and skills, but also feelings and self-image) is necessary.
- Learning is not only the assimilation of knowledge, but also the recognition of what is already known.
- Recognition and revision requires that people should have support from other people with similar problems. Some of these supporting people must come from different settings to help to stimulate the review process. Most of us are open to learning when we receive helpful and accurate feedback from colleagues who are respected, valued and trusted.
- Learning and the revision of our mental sets is made easier in a safe atmosphere. This security develops from skilful preparation and understanding on the part of the facilitator or set adviser and from the support of co-learners.
- Learning only becomes possible when someone both recognizes the need for change and sees the effects of their actions in working on a real problem. We learn best with and from other people, when addressing together pressing problems to which no-one knows the solution. Learning is always for a purpose – resolving a problem or living in a more satisfying way.
- The role of the facilitator of this process is not to teach, but to design, shape and enable conditions out of which people can help each other to understand their own past personal experience and the resulting mental sets. It is about creating a setting in which we feel secure, and so able to review our mental sets, recognize the need for change and see the impact of our actions on real problems.

This all has a number of practical implications:

1 Most people do not approach any problem situation in an academic fashion. They are not so much concerned with a subject or area as with sorting out their current headache.
2 This means that very few of us undertake the pursuit of learning in any 'systematic' way. Instead, learning is limited to the task or problem in hand. Most people, most of the time, use only those parts of any topic or subject which help them to resolve their immediate problem.
3 Learners do not start with the simple and move to the more difficult. Instead they tackle their problems head on. We can cope with complexity and difficulty from the outset provided we can see they are directly relevant to the learning process.
4 It is much easier to recognize and adapt your ideas when you have other people around you, facing similar problems, with whom you can talk.
5 We are looking for an immediate pay-off. Learning we can apply now, rather than in the future.
6 The result of all this is that there is relatively little interest on the part of most learners in general principles. Few people try to draw general conclusions from particular instances. Once the immediate problem has been resolved the tendency is to store how to cope with that specific situation, rather than to generate longer-term and more general learning from it. So learners need help and support (time, structure) which will help them to develop their learning beyond the most immediate and particular.

ORGANIZATIONAL CHANGE

From the organizational change standpoint it is clear that the values, assumptions and beliefs underlying action learning have much in common with organization development (OD). The continuing major text on this field (French and Bell, 1999) identifies a number of assumptions about how organizations work:

- The basic building-blocks of an organization are groups. Therefore the basic units of change are also groups, rather than individuals.
- An important change goal is the reduction of inappropriate conflict between different parts of an organization and the development of more collaborative working.
- Decision-making in successful organizations tends to be located where the information sources are, rather than in a particular role or level of hierarchy.
- Organizations, parts of organizations and individuals continuously manage themselves against goals or objectives.
- One goal of a healthy organization is to develop generally open communication, mutual trust and confidence between and across levels.
- 'People support what they help create.' People affected by a change must be allowed active participation and a sense of ownership in the planning and conduct of the change.

These values can be summed up as trust and respect for the individual, the legitimacy of feelings, open communication, decentralized decision-making, participation and contribution by all organization members, collaboration and co-operation, appropriate uses of power and authentic interpersonal relations.

THE GOALS AND PURPOSES OF ACTION LEARNING

With its roots in adult learning and organizational change it is evident that the goals of action learning are to:

- benefit organizations by addressing perplexing problems that have previously seemed insoluble
- help organizations to use the potential of their staff better
- help individuals to learn with and from others by discussing the difficulties each member of the action learning set experiences while working on an important organizational problem
- benefit individuals by learning how to survive and operate successfully in a complex and confusing world.

Action learning has three mutually reinforcing purposes:

1 To make useful progress on a problem or opportunity in an organization; to make things happen.
2 To help the individual themselves to find out how to deal, in future, with other such ill-defined problems; to help them to learn how to learn.
3 To help those responsible for the development of people in the organization to see their role afresh; that is to help people create the conditions in which they can learn with and from each other in pursuit of a common task. In a practical sense this is the building of a learning organization.

It is what we think we know already that prevents us from learning.

(Claude Bernard)

Chapter 2

Action learning and traditional learning

The future of work consists of *learning* a living.

(Marshall McLuhan)

Part of the attraction of action learning is that it offers a creative alternative to more traditional approaches to learning. Many will be familiar with the vicious learning sequence shown in Figure 2.1.

Figure 2.1 Vicious learning sequence

Training in generalized knowledge and skills

↓

Problems of learning transfer to local situation

↓

Difficulties in application

↓

No rewards for applying the learning

↓

Full stop

Training and education which provides learners with generalized knowledge and skills leaves the problem of transferring these skills and ideas from the classroom or training centre almost entirely to the learner. Typically, the learner experiences difficulty in applying the learning in the work situation where there are little or no rewards (and perhaps even penalties) for trying out new skills. The result is that they grind to a halt.

Action learning provides, instead, a virtuous learning cycle, as shown in Figure 2.2.

In this case, the learning focuses on improving individual and/or organizational effectiveness. As a result, both learner and organization perceive it as relevant and find it easier to apply. This gives them the learning pay-offs they are looking for and their success, in turn, increases their enthusiasm for learning in this way. As Carl Rogers (1961) put it over 40 years ago: 'anything that can be taught to

Figure 2.2 Virtuous learning cycle

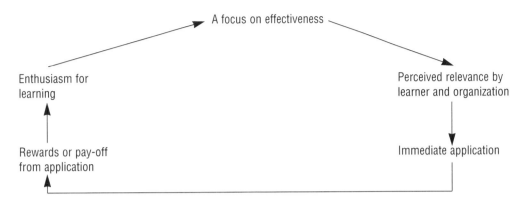

another is relatively inconsequential, and has little or no significant influence on behaviour. The only learning which significantly influences behaviour is self-discovered, self-appropriated learning'.

Bob Garratt (1987) suggests that in work organizations, as in life generally, there is what he calls an 'Action-Fixated Non-Learning Cycle' in operation for most people for most of the time, as shown in Figure 2.3.

Figure 2.3 Action-fixated non-learning cycle

In other words, people observe a situation or problem and, in a 'rush to judgement' immediately devise an explanation or theory which forms the basis of the action they take to deal with the situation or problem. Garratt suggests instead an action learning cycle which interposes the process of reflection at appropriate points, as shown in Figure 2.4.

Figure 2.4 Action learning cycle

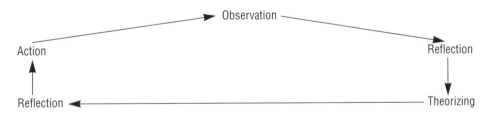

In Garratt's model there is observation, then a pause for reflection, followed by theorizing and then a further reflective pause before taking action.

Michael Eraut (1994) has highlighted four distinct modes in the way learning is used:

1 Replicative: where learning is prepared and packaged for use in situations marked by the completion of routine and repetitive tasks and calling for little exercise of any personal discretion.
2 Applicative: where the emphasis is much more on translating learning into particular prescriptions for action in a variety of different occasions.

3 Interpretative: comprising both understanding (or ways of seeing things from a range of differing perspectives) and judgement or practical wisdom made up of an overall sense of purpose; a feel for appropriateness (what feels right) and a flexibility based on a wealth of personal experience.
4 Associative: in a semiconscious and intuitive manner, involving the use of metaphors and images.

Much traditional learning is concerned only with replicative and applicative usage, but action learning potentially covers the entire continuum, giving as much attention to interpretative and associative learning as to the other modes. The distinction which Eraut also makes between technical knowledge and practical knowledge goes back as far as Aristotle, but reflects the emphasis on practicality and usefulness which lies at the heart of action learning (see Table 2.1).

Table 2.1 Technical and practical knowledge

Technical knowledge is:	Practical knowledge is:
Typically codified and written	Typically expressed in practice and learned only through experience
Based on established practice	Established practice modified by idiosyncratic technique
In accordance with prescription	Loosely, variably, uniquely. In a discretionary way based on personal insight
Used in clearly defined circumstances	Used in both expected and unexpected circumstances
To meet an envisaged and familiar result	To meet an indefinite or novel result
Emphasis on routine (method, analysis, planning)	Emphasis on non-routine (variety, invention and responsiveness)
Focus = well-defined problems	Focus = poorly defined problems

Thus action learning can be seen as a creative alternative to traditional learning. The latter is marked by prescribed, didactic, expert-based transmission of what worked yesterday, while the former emphasizes relevance, usefulness and a concern with what will work today and tomorrow, as shown in Table 2.2.

Table 2.2 Traditional learning and action learning compared

Traditional learning	Action learning
Input based	Output/result based
Learning about others	Learning about self and others
Passive	Active
Individual orientation	Group-based learning
Past orientated	Present and future orientated
Low risk	Higher risk
Arms length	Arm in arm with client
Planning	Planning and doing
Historic case studies	Current real cases
Programmed knowledge (P)	Questioning insight (Q) plus programmed knowledge (P)

Source: Margerison (1988)

Freedom from teachers, from any form of printed syllabus or regulations, from any fixed institution, or even from any literature save the most occasional – not even a case study or a business game!

(Reg Revans)

Chapter 3

Action learning: the root ideas

In a time of profound change, the learners inherit the earth,
While the learned find themselves beautifully equipped
To deal with a world that no longer exists.

(Al Rogers)

Due perhaps to his scientific background Revans expressed the two root ideas of action learning in pseudo-mathematical formulae. The first is

$$L > C$$

where L is the rate of learning and C is the rate of change. In other words, you need to learn faster than things change if you are to have any hope of keeping up. Although such an idea can seem commonplace in the early years of the twenty-first century, it was not so when Revans first formulated it in the 1960s. The 1990s produced an outpouring of ideas and practical methods for developing the learning organization (Senge, 1990; Pedler, Burgoyne and Boydell, 1991; Burgoyne, Pedler and Boydell, 1994; Dixon, 1994) all of which derive from Revans's original insight.

The second formula is

$$L = P + Q$$

where L equals learning, P equals programmed knowledge and Q is questioning insight.

Learning is seen as being made up of two major elements. The first – programmed knowledge – is seen as comprising two elements: external and internal. External programmed knowledge is information and skill pre-packaged for use by learners. It is often contained in a number of products, for example, lectures, handouts, textbooks, manuals, algorithms, checklists, CD-ROMs, computer-assisted learning and so on, which have been produced to capture what has been learned in order to avoid reinventing the wheel. Internal programmed knowledge is made up of our personal mindsets derived from our own experience. An example would be a belief that 'All women bosses are a soft touch'.

Questioning insight, on the other hand, is a process of active listening, questioning and reflecting, leading to review and reinterpretation of our personal experience at the edge of our understanding. An example would be a realization that my own behaviour has produced reactions in others which have locked us all into a problem situation – an understanding that I am part of the problem too. Questioning insight seems to be most useful where there is a limited amount of understanding available around a problem, and where that problem area is rapidly changing. In that sense it is frontier learning or learning on the edge of our understanding.

There is a danger in setting up programmed knowledge and questioning insight as polar opposites. They are both necessary for effective learning. Supplying learners with programmed knowledge which is irrelevant to the problem which they face can be disastrous, but so also is unfocused questioning insight, which can be seen as a form of navel contemplation! One useful way of considering their relationship is shown in Figure 3.1.

Figure 3.1 The relationship between P and Q

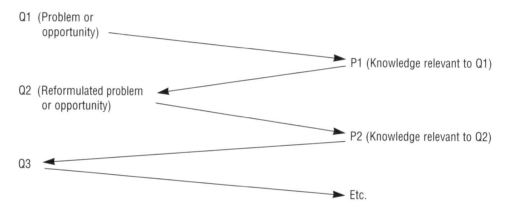

In Figure 3.1 a problem (Q1) is explored and it becomes clear that some programmed knowledge (external or internal) is relevant to addressing the problem. As a result of the application of this (P1) the original problem is reformulated (Q2). In turn, further programmed knowledge (P2) is applied, leading to further clarification of the problem (Q3) and so on. The essence of this is that a problem situation does need the application of relevant programmed knowledge but, importantly, on a just-in-time basis.

The wise see knowledge and action as one.

(Bhagavad-Gita)

Getting the right balance between programmed knowledge and questioning insight is a major challenge. Too much programmed knowledge and not much questioning insight leads to a top-down and didactic delivery of knowledge (and a repetition of the problems identified earlier with traditional learning), while an over-concentration on questioning insight at the expense of programmed knowledge means that people may simply end up reflecting on their reflections without any access to knowledge relevant to their problem situation, in other words, simply pooling their ignorance.

The faster the rate of change which individuals and organizations experience, the faster that programmed knowledge becomes out of date. Therefore, the better our questioning insight (which produces new understanding of the changed situation), the better our chance of personal and organizational survival and growth. This is shown in Figure 3.2.

Figure 3.2 *Programmed knowledge, questioning insight and the rate of change*

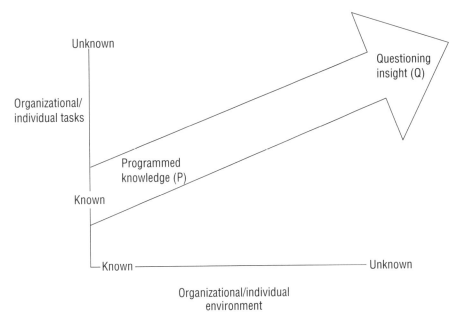

Figure 3.2 suggests that in those situations where the tasks an individual or an organization have to undertake are well known and where the environment or setting in which those tasks are undertaken is familiar, then programmed knowledge will largely suffice, but that where both the environment and the tasks facing organizations and people are unknown, then there is a corresponding greater need for questioning insight. This is the situation facing most people and organizations in the early twenty-first century.

> You always got to be prepared
> But you never know for what.
>
> (Bob Dylan, 'Sugar Baby')

Chapter 4

Balancing learning and task cycles

Responsible action is, in itself, an effective learning process.

(Reg Revans)

Many people recognize that there is a cycle of activity which they follow when they undertake a task or try to solve a problem (see Figure 4.1). After taking some form of action, there are visible results, which they will consider before planning their next action.

Figure 4.1 Task cycle

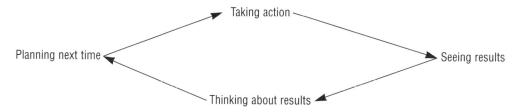

However, taking action and believing that you have learned from it are not the same as taking action and then reviewing that experience in depth and with the help of your colleagues. A second activity cycle – that of learning – is necessary (see Figure 4.2). This activity cycle emphasizes the need to review experience, and conclude what you have learned from it, as the basis for planning what comes next. The reviewing, concluding and thinking about results components of the two cycles are often forgotten or short-circuited in a culture of busyness and in order to get things done. Yet attention to this part of the process is the key to better problem-solving and successful individual learning and development.

Figure 4.2 Learning cycle

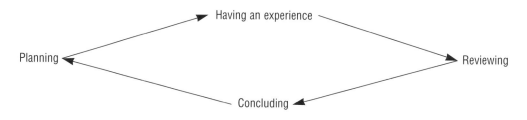

Balancing the task and learning cycles is difficult but can be helped by the idea of 'creative realism' (Finke, 1995), which suggests that there is a growing need to devise solutions to problems which are both creative and realistic. Yet there seem to be two major tensions in operation. The first is between those approaches to problem resolution which are practical and realistic in nature, and those approaches which are seen as more idealistic (radical, aspirational). The other tension is between novel (or previously untried) approaches and more conservative approaches (based largely on the status quo or 'If it ain't bust, why fix it?'). As Figure 4.3 shows, this creates four possible options for action.

Figure 4.3 Dimensions of creative action

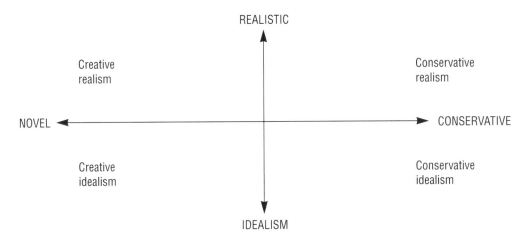

- Conservative realism: related to well-established and more traditional ideas. This approach is very structured and fairly low on imagination and divergent thinking, seeking to avoid any ambiguity and uncertainty. An example of this would be that when faced with an organizational crisis the knee-jerk reaction would be to freeze or cut the training budget.
- Creative idealism: associated with what might be termed 'blue-sky' ideas – trains of thought which are original, but which are often fanciful and unrealistic. Pursuing the same example, faced with the same organizational crisis a 'single-bullet solution' such as training all staff at all levels in the organization in co-counselling as a means of personally coping with the crisis might be implemented.
- Conservative idealism: the extension of common ideas that were unrealistic to begin with, for example, that women are inferior to men. These ideas are likely to be unimaginative with no basis in fact and are often used to close down innovative thinking. In the example given, this might involve scapegoating particular minorities (typically on the basis of race, gender, religion, nationality, and so on) as the cause of the crisis for overspending the training budget.
- Creative realism: showing imagination and divergent thinking, but grounded in real issues and problems. In the same example, faced with the crisis, a representative grouping (perhaps a 'diagonal slice' group) may be set up with time and other support to devise creative routes which see the current financial crisis as offering opportunities, as well as being problematic.

Action learning is concerned with creative realism. It is rooted in the real world but encourages innovative thinking and action to address problems.

The unexamined life is not worth living.

(Socrates)

Part 2

Action Learning in Practice

Chapter 5

Being clear before we begin: groundwork with clients and sponsors

The context for any action learning will be a major factor in success both for individuals and the organization as a whole. A useful first step involves assessing whether the culture or climate of the organization is welcoming (or not) to action learning. There are three helpful tools for doing this: the organizational fitness ranking, the organizational readiness for action learning questionnaire and the organizational learning styles inventory.

The first tool – the organizational fitness ranking (Pedler and Boutall, 1992) – suggests some helpful questions which might be considered by any organization or department before embarking on action learning. It focuses thinking on whether action learning should be used to consolidate existing areas of strength or to address areas of deficit. It can also usefully draw out the different perceptions of different individuals and groups in an organization on such issues.

The second tool is the organizational readiness for action learning questionnaire (Pedler, 1996). Readiness exists when sufficient challenge to the status quo is balanced with an appropriate degree of openness and support. It is often early on in an organization's life cycle (the 'pioneering' phase) when these readiness conditions exist most naturally. As organizations get older, larger and more complex they may lose this natural learning ability. In this questionnaire an organization (or part of an organization) is invited to rate itself against a set of learning organization criteria. This provides a useful guide to the likely value of action learning.

The third approach – the organizational learning styles inventory (Pedler and Aspinwall, 1996) – is based upon a model of organizational learning modes or styles. Using the questionnaire, it is possible to test out the way (or ways) in which an organization as a whole tends to learn, and also to spot which ways of learning are underused. By weighting and distributing scores across a range of statements it is possible to show a preference for, or an underuse of, five styles: habits, memory, imitation, experiment and awareness.

ORGANIZATIONAL FITNESS RANKING

By ranking each item on a scale of 1 to 5 (1 = low, 5 = high) it is possible to highlight those areas in which the organization may be weak, and hence in which effort may need to be focused. No organization is likely to score all 5s or all 1s and, in any case, the ratings are subjective rather than absolute. Action learning cannot be used to rectify major deficiencies in the organization, but it can be helpful in supporting development and growth. It might be a strategic decision, for example, to start action learning in that part of the organization likely to be most supportive of such an approach.

A further way to use the approach might be to get a variety of people in the organization to complete the questionnaire and then compare rankings, thus revealing how different groups of people perceive the same organization. This may help to generate a shared understanding of how the organization functions.

Ranking

1 Purpose/direction
Is there some shared clarity about what the organization is in business for? Do people within the organization have a sense of its purpose and direction – its value, i.e. what is acceptable/legitimate about what we do and how we do it?

_____

2 Individuality
Does the organization value individuality and seek to harness and encourage individual development and interests? (Or is individuality seen as a threat – people must conform?) Can senior people accept that they do not always have all the answers? Can they cope with difficult questions about their decisions?

_____

3 Corporacy
Is there a shared sense of interdependence between the various parts of the organization, so that 'the whole is greater than the sum of the parts'? Do people look for win/win solutions and assess the impact of their actions on other parts of the organization? (Or do they compete regardless of the consequences?)

_____

4 Flexibility
Is the organization flexible? (Or is it excessively hierarchical?) Can it be innovative in the way solutions and ideas are generated across internal boundaries? Does the organization enable and encourage people to take risks? Can and does it respond to new situations quickly and effectively, employing new methods and combinations of skills and experience?

_____

5 Communication
Do open systems of communication exist which ensure that issues and concerns can be aired and shared? Do senior people actively seek out the views of staff and accept criticism constructively? Do systems exist to allow staff to 'whistle-blow' if they see something wrong?

_____

6 Conflict
Does the organization manage conflict? (Or is it suppressed and avoided?) Do people have the opportunity to put their point of view, knowing it will be listened to and taken into account, and are decisions taken overtly and

communicated? (Or are all difficult issues relegated to working parties without clear objectives or timescales?) _____

7 Reward systems

Do reward systems attempt to recognize achievement and contribution? (Or are they based solely on seniority?) Does the organization find ways of rewarding people in ways other than 'pay and rations' (e.g. training and development, flexible working, etc.)? Does the organization celebrate achievement and give clear messages about what constitutes success? _____

8 Organizational learning

Is the organization able to stand back and review its actions and preview the challenges ahead? Does it learn from previous successes and failures – what worked and what didn't? (Or does it stumble and offer knee-jerk reactions to new situations?) Does it have systems to get feedback on its performance? _____

9 Environmentally friendly

Does the organization continually monitor its performance and its relationships with the outside world? Can it anticipate changes in the environment and position itself accordingly? Does it seek to understand how others outside perceive it? _____

Source: Pedler (1996). Reproduced with the kind permission of Lemos & Crane, London.

ORGANIZATIONAL READINESS FOR ACTION LEARNING QUESTIONNAIRE

The questionnaire helps to assess the chance of action learning working in your organization. For each statement score the organization from 1 (not much like us) to 5 (very like us).

Score

In this organization

• People are rewarded for asking good questions	1 2 3 4 5
• People often come up with new ideas	1 2 3 4 5
• There is a fairly free flow of communications	1 2 3 4 5
• Conflict is surfaced and dealt with rather than suppressed	1 2 3 4 5
• We are encouraged to learn new skills	1 2 3 4 5
• We take time out to reflect on experiences	1 2 3 4 5
• There are plenty of books, videos, packages and other resources for learning	1 2 3 4 5
• People help, encourage and constructively criticize each other	1 2 3 4 5
• We are flexible in our working patterns and used to working on several jobs at once	1 2 3 4 5
• Senior people never pull rank and always encourage others to speak their minds	1 2 3 4 5

Now total the scores. If you score:

Between 10 and 20   Action learning probably won't work in your organization until things open up a bit more.

Between 21 and 40   Yes, action learning should work well to help you achieve your purposes.

Over 40   You don't need action learning – or maybe action learning would help you to develop your critical faculties?

Used with the author's permission.

ORGANIZATIONAL LEARNING STYLES INVENTORY

The questionnaire takes the form of seven incomplete sentences, each of which has five possible completing statements. For each of the incomplete sentences, there are 12 points to allocate among the five statements accompanying it, depending on how typical of your organization you think it is. For example, if you think that the first of the five absolutely describes your organization, while none of the other four does at all, then you could give 12 points to that number 1 statement. More likely you will want to distribute your 12 points among the five, giving most points to that which best describes your organization and few or no points to that which least describes your organization. The more you are able to discriminate, the clearer will be the organizational learning style of your organization.

A: In this organization, we are really good at

1 Operating to standard procedures   _____

2 Collecting and storing knowledge and data   _____

3 Benchmarking best practice from other organizations   _____

4 Innovating and finding new ways of doing things   _____

5 Being critically aware of what is going on in our world   _____

Total points: *12*

B: The most respected people in this organization are those who

1 Do things according to the book   _____

2 Know a great deal about our business   _____

3 Bring in lots of new ideas from other organizations   _____

4 Develop new ideas and practices on the job   _____

5. Are always asking questions about the way we do things   _____

Total points: *12*

C: What we're most likely to say about ourselves is that we have

1 First-class operating systems   _____

2 Databases and information back-up unmatched in our field   _____

3 Excellent networking with other organizations   _____

4 An experimental, 'leading-edge' reputation   _____

5 Wide vision and take a long view   _____

Total points: *12*

D: What we're least likely to say is

1 'No one sings from the same hymn-sheet.'   _____

2 'History is bunk.'   _____

3 'We've got nothing to learn from the opposition.'   _____

4 'If it ain't broke, don't fix it.'   _____

5 'Go for the quick fix every time.'   _____

Total points: *12*

E: When there's a crisis we

1 Remain calm and continue with the correct procedure   ————

2 Search for data and precedents we can learn from   ————

3 Ring round our contacts and ask their advice   ————

4 Drop everything else and get stuck in – we love it!   ————

5 Act only after mature consideration of the wider implications of

   possible actions   ————

Total points: *12*

F: Our biggest weakness is

1 Getting stuck in fixed ways of responding   ————

2 Depending on things that worked well for us in the past   ————

3 Relying too much on other people's ideas   ————

4 Reinventing everything – even when they work OK   ————

5 Losing clear, short-term focus   ————

Total points: *12*

G: The most pressing priority for change in this organization is to

1 Loosen up and give people more discretion and responsibility   ————

2 Develop a future orientation and vision   ————

3 Encourage people inside to develop their own ideas   ————

4 Strengthen operating procedures and cut down on experiment for

   experiment's sake   ————

5. Balance short- and long-term foci   ————

Total points: *12*

Scoring: Transfer your total points for each sentence to the table.

	1	2	3	4	5
A					
B					
C					
D					
E					
F					
G					
Totals					

The higher your score for 1, 2, 3, 4 or 5, the more your organization tends to use this style of learning according to your responses.

The lower your score for 1, 2, 3, 4 or 5, the less your organization tends to use this style of learning according to your responses.

The numbers 1, 2, 3, 4 and 5 correspond to the following organizational learning styles:

1 **Habits:** These are the 'standard operating procedures' or 'conditioned reflexes', the enduring 'wired-in' reactions which are capable of surviving the loss or departure of particular individuals. Valuable though this style can be it can also degenerate into a simple unthinking repetition of familiar responses to novel situations and problems, producing sterility and rigidity of thought and action.

2 **Memory:** Or an emphasis on accumulated and 'stored' experience – databases, product or market knowledge, technical 'know-how', etc. – often contained in people's heads, invisible and uncollected and thus seldom subject to scrutiny and challenge. The downside of this style is that this represents a past-orientated culture ('What worked yesterday will also work today – and tomorrow too') and very resistant to change.

3 **Imitation:** Or 'modelling best practice'. This organizational learning style involves copying others (e.g. market leaders) and in benchmarking against the best. Seeking out and adopting good practice from competitors and/or partners is a positive approach and generally to be welcomed, but this may sometimes degenerate into a 'flavour of the month' or quick-fix orientation with a corresponding lack of belief in any internal ability to innovate – good ideas always come from without, never from within. There is also a danger of 'walking backwards into the future' by concentrating on what is good practice now, but in fact really copying yesterday's successes.

4 **Experiment:** An organizational learning style of innovating through continuous trial and error by piloting new initiatives and actively experimenting with new ways of doing things – getting feedback, reflecting on success and failure and forming new ideas. This can be a valuable style but the danger is one of 'initiative-itis' – the generation of too many ideas and a failure to 'harvest' them and realize their potential, leading to a tendency to be perceived as 'change junkies'.

5 **Awareness:** An organizational learning style marked by an openness and a continuous and critical questioning of self, organization, partner organizations and the wider environment in terms of purpose, direction, whether ends justify means, etc. The downside of such a style can be a loss of focus and a lack of attention to business detail – perhaps even a loss of interest in the business.

A large score for one of the five styles suggests an organizational preference for that way of doing things, while a low score indicates that this way of learning is underused. A fairly even distribution of points could suggest that the organization is balanced and multiskilled at learning, although it might also mean that it does not really have any learning strengths at all – just that you had to allocate the points somewhere!

The questionnaire has to be used in a thoughtful way – perhaps to check against other evidence or as the basis for a discussion on learning and development vis-à-vis organizational performance.

Source: Pedler and Aspinwall (1996). The material is reproduced with the kind permission of McGraw-Hill Publishing Company.

Chapter 6

Preparing for an action learning programme

> If I continue to believe as I have always believed,
> I will continue to act as I have always acted;
> And if I continue to act as I have always acted,
> I will continue to get what I have always got.
>
> (Marilyn Ferguson)

Setting up an action learning programme requires careful groundwork if it is to have a realistic chance of success. Preparation is crucial to the success of action learning.

Before anything begins in the organization you need to:

- read a fair amount of material about action learning, especially case studies of action learning set meetings, in order to get a feel for what goes on there
- talk to people who have been members of action learning sets or who have acted as facilitators or set advisers
- gain some personal experience in action learning, preferably by being a member of an action learning set.

BEGINNINGS

Usually a 'mover and shaker' or 'product champion' in the organization will initiate or trigger the action learning programme. This might be a human resource or training person or someone in a leadership role. It is usual for this person to develop a basic plan and then take it for discussion with other stakeholders in the organization in order to develop ownership. These stakeholders are likely to include:

- senior people in the organization, particularly the chief executive
- middle-level managers or professional staff, who will be responsible for the areas in which the action learning programme might operate and who may have to arrange cover for their staff involved in action learning set meetings (and also the work they undertake between these meetings)
- potential action learning set members
- the potential set advisers or facilitators.

There are two main ways in which the idea may be taken forward by the initial product champion – either:

1 Brainstorming the as yet unresolved (but burning) issues which face the organization and identify the leading-edge ones. Action learning works best in dealing with the unknown.
2 Prioritizing a list of likely areas to address.
3 Selecting a workplace theme, topic or project which has to be dealt with anyway and about which no one really knows what to do. It must be challenging and delve into the unknown in order to offer the learning required.
4 Developing a draft proposal to present to the wider stakeholder group.

or:

1 Enlisting stakeholder support by asking for volunteers to work on the above, using this to model the activity of an action learning set.

Some questions which might usefully be addressed at this stage include:

- Will the theme, topic or project choice involve participants in significant change?
- Is what is being proposed feasible in terms of the timescale, resources, experience and skills available?
- Are the risks of failure high enough to stimulate action, without being too threatening?
- Is the problem/issue unknown enough to require imaginative and creative solutions?
- Will the problem/issue expose participants to different perspectives and ways of learning?
- Are senior people in the organization really committed to the success of the programme?
- Does the organization have the power and the will to implement changes arising from the action learning process?

If ownership of the programme is to be established and then maintained, the stakeholders will need to be systematically and continually informed, in plain English, about:

- the concept of action learning
- what it will mean for them
- the type and length of commitment and support which they will need to provide.

This marketing function is important. For the duration of the programme regular internal communication and the continuous selling of the concept to the stakeholders so that they feel included will serve to reinforce how action learning works and deal with any confusion or misconceptions which may arise.

Activity is the only road to knowledge.

(George Bernard Shaw)

Chapter 7

Action learning problems and projects: type and selection

A problem is an opportunity in work clothes.

(Henry Kaiser)

Although action learning is about the learning and development of people, it is also about the solving of problems in work organizations. Bob Garratt suggests that there are two major inputs needed for the problem-solving process to be successful – hard (or technical) inputs and soft (or socio-emotional) inputs. Hard inputs are about problem resolution, task achievement, efficient resource use, the bottom line and the meeting of targets and objectives. They emphasize the need to be logical, rational, quantifying and structuring and are expressed in debate, challenge and constructive criticism.

Soft inputs relate to personal feelings, drives and motivations, and emphasize the importance of relationships and the need for a safe and secure setting, and peer support in which personal experience can be reviewed and reinterpreted.

The two inputs are complementary and cannot be separated from each other, and in action learning they are not, as shown in Figure 7.1.

Figure 7.1 Inputs to the problem-solving process

PROBLEMS

Words like problem, project, issue and theme are all used loosely here quite deliberately. Some people also dislike the use of the term problem and prefer to use opportunity. Whatever it is called in the organization, it will be the primary vehicle for action and learning, so it must be demanding without being overwhelming. It must address an unresolved issue at job, team, departmental, interdepartmental, professional, interprofessional, organizational or interorganizational level. Tackling the problem will not only move the present situation forward, but will also contribute to individual and group learning about how work is done on other problems.

In choosing areas to address, it seem sensible that:

- the areas to be addressed are important to the organization and are not contrived exercises
- the areas chosen are complex in nature, dealing with problems which extend across various parts of the organization
- they are not amenable to expert solutions, nor have any ready-made right answers.

PROBLEMS AND PUZZLES

Revans originally made the useful distinction between puzzles and problems. Puzzles have best solutions and right and wrong answers which people have to discover. Puzzles are organizational embarrassments which can be solved via the application of programmed knowledge[1] alone (often with the help of experts). Devising a business plan for a department within a tightly structured organization is likely to be only a puzzle, especially if it happens where the organization provides staff with highly specific guidance on business planning, based on a standardized format and within clearly defined and tight resource constraints.

By contrast problems are messy, complex, dynamic and interdependent tangles which have no right answers and no existing single solution. Problems can be tackled by different individuals in different circumstances and in different ways. For a company to decide to enter a new market with a new product would be a real problem, which would need to be addressed by using questioning insight[2], together with just-in-time programmed knowledge.

Problems are issues which, if not tackled properly, will escalate. They are topics about which (at least some) key stakeholders in the organization care strongly. Therefore, problems should:

- be real and significant: key stakeholders must care about the area in question. Failure to address the area is likely to provoke a crisis. Ideally, the area should also be critical and urgent, but experience shows that the tendency is often to not entrust such immediate issues to the part-time members of action learning sets and to choose instead issues which are medium to long term in nature. Whatever the area you choose, it should be something which participants can 'get their teeth into'.

---

[1] Programmed knowledge: either our personal mindsets drawn from our earlier lived experience or pre-packaged information and theories devised by others.
[2] Questioning insight: new understanding gained from listening, questioning and reflection, leading to review and reinterpretation of experience.

- involve the participant in action (implementation) as well as diagnosis: participants should be required not only to diagnose and propose solutions to problems, but also become involved in the (often infinitely messier) business of putting proposals into effect. This has implications for the timescale of the action learning programme and the timescale for diagnosing and resolving the problem, and the effective dove-tailing of each. Ideally the problem should lie within the participants' sphere of responsibility or they should be given the authority to take matters to a conclusion.
- be a challenge: the problem area should be something new which participants have not previously addressed and which they both want and are able to resolve.
- be defined in some way: problem areas may be either tightly or loosely-defined. Whatever the style of definition, all participants will need to address such basic questions such as '*Whose* problem is this?', '*Why* is it seen as a problem?' and 'Is the problem as presented symptomatic of something deeper?' Beyond this some projects will be *tightly-defined* either in terms of the time available to address them or in the light of the abilities and learning needs of participants. An example here might be the merging of two work units within a prescribed time-period. Other projects will be *loosely-defined* and this may help the participant, particularly if they come from a professional or technical background with a particular 'mind-set' and a tendency to see problems in a specific way. The more loosely-defined and open-ended project may encourage this person to cope with differing perspectives and learn to live with a greater degree of ambiguity than previously, thus preparing them for future challenges. A loosely-defined project might involve the exploration of a potential new market niche.
- be capable of being learned from: participants should be able to report-back at Action Learning set meetings on progress (action) and personal insight (learning). The issue chosen should not be so specialised and obtuse that the other set members do not feel able to challenge and support the participant in the way they address the problem.

> It isn't that they can't see the solution,
> It is that they can't see the problem.

(G.K. Chesterton)

PROBLEMS: FAMILIAR AND UNFAMILIAR

Problems can be seen as a combination of either familiar or unfamiliar tasks and familiar or unfamiliar settings, as shown in Figure 7.2.

Figure 7.2 Task/setting matrix

		TASK	
		Familiar	Unfamiliar
S E T T I N G	Familiar	1	2
	Unfamiliar	3	4

Figure 7.2 contains four cells.

In Cell 1 someone stays in post within their current job and tackles a familiar problem. There is an ever-present danger here that the issue chosen either is really a puzzle rather than a problem or has been contrived just for the purposes of the action learning programme and so does not really contain the challenge needed.

In Cell 2 a person stays in their present job but tackles an issue which they have never previously addressed within their work role – something novel and challenging.

In Cell 3 someone tackles an issue which they have previously had some success in resolving in their day job, but now they are faced with the challenge of trying to repeat this success in a new department or organization where they are unfamiliar with the history, culture and ways of working.

In Cell 4 someone moves to another organization (or an unfamiliar part of their own organization) and tackles an unusual and previously unfamiliar problem.

Most typical problems which people are likely to address as part of an action learning programme are either those within their own job or elsewhere in their own organization (Cells 1 and 2). But action learning is not confined to this focus. Many successful action learning programmes have been interorganizational in both the private sector and between parts of the public sector. For example, the Brighton Health Care National Health Service (NHS) Trust and the Brighton Council Social Services Departments jointly devised and ran an action learning programme which involved action learning sets comprising people from both organizations who undertook unfamiliar projects in the other organization (Cell 4).

Finally, action learning programme participants can benefit from focused thinking on what problem, opportunity or issue they wish to address. Sometimes it is difficult to choose between a number of possibilities. Using the task/setting matrix shown in Figure 7.2 can help, but so can the following questions contained in the action learning problem brief (Pedler and Boutall, 1992):

1 Describe your problem situation in one sentence.
2 Why is this important?
   To you?
   To your organization?
3 How will you recognize progress on this problem?
4 Who else would like to see progress on this problem?
5 How do you intend to go about tackling this problem? What will be your first steps?
6 What difficulties do you anticipate?
7 What are the benefits if this problem is reduced or resolved?
   To you?
   To your organization?

(Used with authors' permission.)

The work will teach you how to do it.

(Estonian proverb)

Chapter 8

Action learning sets: composition

Coming together is the beginning.
Keeping together is progress.
Working together is success.

(Henry Ford)

Action learning sets are the main vehicle for learning and action and central to how action learning works. They are:

- concerned with helping members learn from the problems which they are solving, so they tend to challenge people's assumptions and confront their actions
- concerned with implementing your solutions as well as diagnosis or planning
- focused on unfamiliar problems, rather than on problems in which the members already have experience.

Action learning sets exist as the means by which individual members work out and pursue their own actions in the workplace and learn from that experience through a process of review, reflection and planning.

CRITERIA FOR SET MEMBERSHIP

Four criteria are important when planning an action learning set – interest, diversity, equality and challenge.

Interest: participation in an action learning set should be voluntary, wherever possible, because personal motivation plays a significant role in sustaining effort. This means that capturing the interest of each participant is vital. Potential set members should recognize that a problem exists, should want to tackle it and should see the set as a potential useful support in doing so.

Diversity: personal qualities and skills, together with a variety of organizational, departmental and professional experiences and styles create a rich mixture for the set. Sufficient contrast is needed to provide grit in the oyster of the set, but too great a diversity may create problems. The group may find it hard to form and develop a shared sense of identity.

Equality is important. The group should share a broadly common age range and work experience, together with broadly the same level of career progression and achievement. Generally the intellectual and emotional capacity of set members should be similar because it is important so that no set member ever feels out of their depth.

Level of challenge: the challenge inherent in the problem should be broadly similar for all set members. Problems should be:

- real and significant
- involve action as well as diagnosis
- not previously addressed
- defined in some way
- capable of being learned from.

ALTERNATIVE GROUPINGS

Sets should comprise around a maximum of seven or eight people. A set may be made up of members drawn from all levels within the same function – a vertical grouping, for example, the sales director, area sales managers and geographically based salesmen. This type of set shows evidence of strong support and commitment from the organization or function and promotes the notion of equality of contribution from all individuals. A vertical grouping allows a full spectrum of views and opinions on particular issues and provides a ready-made means of communication between all the organizational levels concerned, thus making the likelihood of action much more certain. If there are over-hierarchical or dominant relationships already in existence, then such vertical groupings may serve to stifle members' input. Difficulties in communicating ideas and concerns may also occur, due to differences in both perspective and ability.

Horizontal groupings are made up of people working at a similar level in one, or across a number of, organizations. Examples here might be executive directors of NHS Trusts or local authority directors of Social Services. In this case the shared experience and common ground may help reduce barriers and encourage greater levels of trust. The set may find it easier to establish agreed social processes and feel more comfortable in offering spirited challenge.

On the other hand, if people's perspectives are fairly similar and set members are happy with such established patterns then it may be harder to shake or challenge shared views. In such circumstances any power games between set members will be quite subtle, difficult to spot and tricky to deal with.

A Combination grouping involves mixing these two major types together.

QUESTIONS ABOUT SET MEMBERSHIP

Questions worth asking when considering membership of a set include:

- Is there anyone missing who could really contribute to the work of the set?
- Will everyone who is interested in being a set member be allowed to attend set meetings or will they be subject to pressure or criticism for doing so?

- Will there be all-male, all-female or mixed gender sets?
- What will be the maximum and minimum numbers in the sets?
- Who is it important to have in the sets?

The answers to these questions will vary according to the project/issue being addressed and the overall intentions of the programme.

Do not forget the question of the consistency of the set membership. It is often impossible for every set member to attend every meeting, but more than one absence of any one member can hold back the effectiveness of the set. Checking-out other potential pressures on set members at the outset can be a useful screening activity.

Chapter 9

Action learning sets: agreeing groundrules

At the beginning of the life of the set you will need to establish groundrules to govern the behaviour of the set members, to allay any fears that people may have about what might happen and to establish and model shared responsibility and joint working between the set members and the set adviser. Groundrules are typically both practical and behavioural in nature.

Practical groundrules should cover such matters as:

- Life expectancy of the set – how long will it continue to meet?
- Frequency and duration of set meetings – how often, and for how long on each occasion, should it meet?
- Format for meetings and how time will be allocated.

Behavioural groundrules should address such issues as:

- commitment and priority: set members will be busy people with many calls on their time. To attend set meetings and to engage fully in the life of the set takes a degree of commitment and an agreement to make set meetings (and what goes on between them) a priority. It involves a self-discipline among set members which it is important to address right at the start of the set's life.
- confidentiality: while almost all set members are likely to subscribe to this in principle, it is an important job for the set adviser to help the set members to tease out exactly what is meant in practice by this term. Confidentiality cannot ever be absolute, so the aim should be to establish the limits of confidentiality and to agree on the circumstances when set members (and the set adviser) might communicate information to people outside the set. It is vitally important that these circumstances are clear to every set member, since this allows them to make an informed choice about exactly what they disclose in the set.
- timekeeping: to ensure that each person has a fair share of the time available for their issues, it will be important to keep to both the external time boundaries of the meeting (that is, starting and finishing on time) and the internal boundaries (the amount of time allocated to each set member).
- equal air-time: only one person at a time is the problem-holder. For the duration of their time the other set members are there to listen and to enable the problem-holder to resolve the problem. If the problem-holder is not getting the sort of help needed, then he or she should say so! It will be important to

agree to avoid anecdotes or other set members' parallel problems. Examples would be:

- 'I have a similar problem in my department.'
- 'I had difficulties with Y when she worked for me.'
or
- 'We all know what the chief executive is like!'

- openness: the success of the set will turn to a great extent upon the degree to which set members feel comfortable enough to be open with one another. A groundrule which involves saying 'I' when you mean 'I', rather than 'one', 'we' or 'you' will ensure that people own their statements.
- enabling behaviour: the set members are there to help the problem-holder to find his or her best possible course of action, not to offer their own solutions, unless requested to do so by the problem-holder as part of a brainstorm of possibilities. 'Only in a group where it is safe to disclose ignorance, admit weakness and ask for help is it possible for the problem-holder to learn at sufficient depth for him or her to develop as an individual' (Gaunt and Kendall, 1985). The set should provide a safe and experimental space where each person can take the risk of trying out new ways of relating to others, knowing that they will get constructive feedback and not be blamed for getting it wrong.

A set of groundrules for an action learning set might look something like this:

- Make attendance at set meetings a priority (except for sickness or emergencies).
- Contact the set adviser if I cannot attend a set meeting.
- Arrange in my absence for my contribution to be reported by another set member.
- Make every effort to complete the actions that we have identified we will take between set meetings.
- Inform the set adviser if such actions cannot be taken.
- Actively listen to what other set members say.
- Maintain confidentiality, especially when private or personal matters are discussed in the set.
- Participate with enthusiasm.
- Question my own, and each others', assumptions.
- Reflect on my own learning in review sessions or learning diaries.
- Take responsibility for the project outcome and my own learning.
- Roughly equal air-time.
- Speak in plain English – no jargon.
- No blame is attached to asking what a word, phrase or abbreviation means.

The exact number of groundrules decided upon is not important and will vary from set to set. It is probably more important to agree on five groundrules that set members will stick to rather than 25 that they will not! The most important groundrule is the one which says that all groundrules are open to renegotiation and that new rules can be established any time that the set feels it is necessary.

DEVISING GROUNDRULES

Guidelines for the process to follow in creating groundrules are given in more detail in *The Facilitator's Toolkit* (Havergal and Edmonstone, 1999) but typically involve:

- seeking suggestion from set members
- encouraging debate about what they mean
- writing-up agreed groundrules on a flipchart
- either posting the flipchart at every set meeting in full view of set members, or having groundrules typed, copied and distributed to all set members – or both
- pointing out that groundrules can be added to or renegotiated as the life of the set progresses, and allowing time for this to happen
- using the groundrules as part of the review process at the end of set meetings.

Chapter 10

Action learning set meetings

Tell me, I'll forget.
Show me, I may remember.
Involve me and I'll understand.

(Chinese proverb)

LOCATION AND VENUE

Where the set meets is important. A quiet, well-ventilated and adequately heated room is the minimum requirement. Seating should be comfortable and, if possible, all the chairs should be of roughly the same design and arranged in a circle. Coffee-making facilities, flipchart pads and pens and so on should also be on hand.

When set meetings take place in work organizations there is always the possibility of interruptions, so a groundrule covering this may be necessary. Alternatively, the set might opt for a less convenient but neutral venue to which some of the set members might have to travel (and which might involve extra cost). If the set involves people from a variety of locations there may be value in moving the venue around so that each set member can act as host or hostess, although beware the danger of competition over provision of lunches!

Central to considerations about the venue of set meetings is the issue of boundary protection – of ensuring that set members feel that they are operating in a safe and supportive environment where they feel reasonably comfortable in addressing their workplace and problem-related concerns. The set acts as a holding environment or transitional space in which participants handle their anxiety, so the extent to which the set is able to exclude the immediate demands and pressures of the set members' work environments and create a space which is truly the set's own for the duration of the set meeting – without any intrusion of work pressures – is likely to be a key to its success.

ACTIVITIES

Five major activities occur in action learning set meetings:

1 Members share their perspectives on the problems being tackled.

2 Members support and challenge each other in understanding the problem, generating actions and understanding the learning that occurs in tackling the problem.
3 Set members question each other's current understanding of the problem, question their own perceptions and discover the insights that result from posing fresh questions.
4 The set develops over time; it forms, matures and learns how to work together creatively and productively.
5 The set reviews (evaluates) how well the set and its members are operating.

Set meetings typically go through a number of stages:

- Catching up: this can serve to allow each member to share their immediate or 'hot' news and helps to reintegrate the group. Sometimes a warm-up exercise might be used for similar purposes, especially in the early days of the set.
- Agenda-setting: in some instances this will simply involve confirming the format previously agreed at the last set meeting or modifying it. In other cases the set members will set the agenda, agree the running order and allocate the time available, there and then. While in principle all members have equal 'air-time' this may be modified by agreement, according to need or urgency.
- Progress reporting: each set member has a time slot and takes it in turn to report on progress made with their project or issue since the last set meeting and the state of the problem as it stands now. There are a number of key questions which set members can usefully address here and these are identified in the section 'Key questions in action learning'.

The more that set members can think things through, in advance of set meetings; structure their time well within their time slot; specify clearly what they want the set to focus on; ask for what they want and end by generating action points for themselves, the more they will benefit from the set's work.

Set members have a range of options for using the slot. They could, for example:

- Ask the other set members to stay quiet while they give a short presentation, and then ask for comments.
- Have a pre-prepared flipchart itemizing the key points they want to address, or capture them on the flipchart in real time.
- Ask the other participants to brainstorm possible ways of tackling a problem they face.
- Ask the other set members to discuss the problem as presented, while taking personal notes of useful ideas that emerge.
- Tape-record the time slot and play it back later.

- The meeting focuses on each set member and their problem in turn, supporting, challenging and questioning, and offering resources of various types (contacts, material, sources and so on), the other set members helping the problem-holder to learn from what has happened and to find a way forward for the next period.
- Review: at the end of each set meeting some time for reflection, feedback and discussion on individual and group processes is valuable. The latter should focus on such questions as 'What worked well today?', 'What was a problem in this meeting?' or 'How can we be more effective next time?'

At the core of set meetings are the twin activities of support and challenge. Support (or emotional warmth) cannot be simply engineered and may take time to build, although skilled facilitation by the set adviser (and by set members) can accelerate the process. An appropriate degree of support is often needed before challenge can be accepted. Challenge involves questioning and questions may be either helpful or unhelpful.

QUESTIONS

Unhelpful questions include:

- Closed questions: these can only be answered by a 'Yes' or a 'No'; they curtail the set members' options for responding. They usually begin with a 'Do you...?', an 'Are you...?' or a 'Have you...?'
- Leading/loaded questions: these are questions which put the answer into the other set members' mouths. They usually demonstrate what the person asking them already knows (or think they know) rather than what the problem-holder really understands or believes.
- Multiple questions: several questions rolled into one – people will inevitably choose the easiest answers first and avoid the difficult question which is part of the 'package'.
- Long-winded questions: these will probably be misunderstood.
- Overly probing questions: questions that the set member is not ready to answer, given the level of maturity and trust in the set.
- Too many questions: conducting an interrogation will lead to defensiveness.
- Poorly timed questions: questions that interrupt the set members from doing their own work on the problem and come at the wrong time in the helping process.
- Trick questions: which are likely to cause resentment, demotivation and even withdrawal.

By contrast, other questions can be helpful:

- Open questions: aimed at provoking an extended free response. They might start with 'What', 'Where', 'Which', 'Why', 'How' or 'When'.
- Awareness-raising questions: questions like 'How did it feel when you were doing that?' or 'What do you imagine it would look like if you did it differently?' encourage self-awareness and focus on positive ideas for future action.
- Elaborating questions: these give the problem-holder the opportunity to expand on what they have already started talking about. Examples are 'Could you say some more about that?' or 'Could you amplify what you've just said?'
- Reflective questions: these help to get clarification by replaying the problem-holder's words or rephrasing and reflecting them back in order to both test understanding and encourage the problem-holder to talk more. Examples are 'So what you're saying is...' or 'Let me check I'm understanding you correctly...'.
- Specification questions: these aim to get more detail about the problem, for example, 'When you say he upsets you, what precisely happens?', 'When?' or 'How many times?'
- Justifying questions: these provide an opportunity for further explanation of reasons, attitudes or feelings. Examples are 'How would you explain that to someone else?' or 'Could you help me to understand by putting it another way?'
- Focusing on feelings questions: these questions aim to tease out the emotions generated by the problem. These should be open and tentative since the

problem-holder should (but does not always) know his or her own feelings better than anyone else. Examples here include 'How do you feel about that?' and 'I seem to hear you saying that you feel...'.

- Personal ownership questions: these imply not only that the problem-holder has a responsibility for owning the problem, but also for making the choices that contribute to its solution. They aim to establish links between how the problem-holder initially describes the problem and his or her role in sustaining or resolving it. Examples include 'How do you see your own behaviour contributing to this situation?' and 'Are there any ways in which you might be helping yourself more?'
- Hypothetical questions: these pose a situation or suggestion – 'What if?' or 'How about?' – and can be useful for introducing a new idea or concept or challenging a response.
- Checking questions: this is checking to what is being heard or correcting an understanding, for example, 'Is this always truc in every situation?'
- Incisive questions: the first part of an incisive question asserts a positive assumption, while the second directs the problem-holder's attention back to the issue or goal. Examples include 'If you were told that your job depended on changing the way that you worked, what would you do first?', 'If you were in charge of things round here, what would you tackle first and how would you go about it?' and 'If things could be exactly right for you in this situation, how would they have to change?'

Useful questions derived from the experience of action learning sets are contained in the section 'Key questions in action learning'. The aim in all circumstances is to find and use those questions which lead the problem-holder to question him or herself – the process which fosters questioning insight. A good question is selfless. It is not asked in order to highlight how clever the questioner is or to generate more information (or an interesting response) for the questioner. Rather it is a means of opening up the problem-holder's own view of the problem, issue or situation.

APPROPRIATE ATTITUDES AND BEHAVIOUR

Experience suggests that there are appropriate attitudes and behaviours which foster productive working in action learning sets (Beaty, Bourner and Frost, 1993).

Helpful attitudes include:

- Concern for the well-being of fellow set members: set members need to care enough about their fellow set members to want them to succeed with their project or problem and to learn from that experience.
- Each set member is the world expert on their own problem: problem-holders will always have access to information which they do not (either by choice or circumstance) convey to the other set members. Thus, only by believing that people can help themselves can effective help be given. Respect is needed for the judgement of fellow set members to identify what they can and cannot use from the set's discussion.
- Empathy: a willingness to share another's feelings and thoughts – to say to oneself 'What does it feel like to be *that* person with *that* problem?' – an attitude which is curious and thoughtful about the problem-holder and their problem, sometimes described as 'intelligent naivety'.

Derived from this, helpful behaviours include:

- Challenging: by questioning – see above.
- Supporting: providing a shoulder to lean on, both in the set meetings and between them (by telephone calls, emails, providing contacts, materials and so on).
- Conveying empathy: this is a powerful means of giving the problem-holder permission to share more.
- Learning not to interrupt: jotting down ideas with a pen and paper to contribute later can help this process.
- Active listening (to what set members say) and attending (to the non-verbal cues) will ensure full and close attention.
- Continually asking 'Is this helpful?'

ENDINGS

While most action learning sets are initiated for an agreed and finite time period, there is often a strong urge on the part of the set members for the life of the set to continue. This may be because, for some set members, the combination of support and challenge which they receive from colleagues is fairly unique in relation to the remainder of their work or life experience. Yet action learning sets are not permanent entities and the members (and the issues which these members address) will change over time.

Given the level of commitment required of set members, any set will need to review regularly whether it is continuing to meet individual needs and there will inevitably come a time when that particular configuration of people, competence and issues are no longer effective for each member. Sets which continue to meet either out of habit or because it is comfortable to do so will not be productive.

So ending the life of the set should not be seen as a failure. It is a good test of action learning itself – the group needs to know when to stop, rather than continue on in a sterile manner. If the set has been working well it will be mature enough to realize that as much has been achieved as can be achieved and that the time has come to stop. The ending of the set is thus part of the process of development – a symbol of growth rather than loss.

The final session of a set might well include the following four tasks, instigated by the set adviser:

1 Set members quietly and personally recapture the way they felt when first coming to the set.
2 Set members reflect on the aims and outcomes of the set by discovering what each member has achieved since the set started, and hence remind themselves just how far they have come.
3 Set members reflect on the experience of being in the set by remembering how it had been along the way.
4 Members notice and share with each other (and the set adviser) how they are now feeling at the end of the set's life, and say their goodbyes before moving on.

Ultimately, though, the set adviser must put her faith in the set members to say goodbye as they see fit. Some sets do this in a flood of emotion, while others simply retire to the pub with very little fuss!

The processes which set members have gone through and the relationships which they have built, fostered and maintained will prove valuable to them after the set has finished, in a variety of different settings. The lessons learned by set members will continue long after the set itself has gone.

> Alone we can do so little; together we can do so much.
>
> (Helen Keller)

SELF-FACILITATED SETS

Most action learning sets have a set adviser or facilitator working with them for the duration of the programme. This is because his or her expertise can be essential in the early life of the set and because there is a tendency for set members to become engrossed with the action at the expense of the learning, and the set adviser can act as a necessary corrective to this tendency.

Yet the ultimate goal of set advisers must be to make themselves redundant as the set members become more mature and experienced in working together. The set adviser might, for example, ask the set members to review the set adviser role and how it is working out after an agreed number of meetings. If the role became less and less necessary it may be sensible for the set adviser to attend set meetings by invitation only – as and when the set membership feel that it would be necessary and helpful to the learning process of the group.

There will be some situations where the membership of a set is sufficiently experienced and mature (perhaps from earlier membership of other sets) that they can operate in a self-facilitating manner. However, to do so demands:

- a high personal commitment from all the set members to attend and to share the work of facilitation as agreed
- clear agreement among set members about the format to be followed for set meetings and clarity over roles. For example, will each set member take it in turn at different meetings to act as facilitator or will this be undertaken collectively?
- a high degree of honesty in undertaking the review of each set meeting so that the set does not, for example, collude to ignore unhelpful behaviour.

> Thus we may more accurately describe action learning as development of the self by the mutual support of equals.
>
> (Reg Revans)

Chapter 11

Learning and development in action learning: the energy investment model

Set members bring to their membership of the set a combination of energy and attitude, and this produces individual styles of behaviour, rather than types of people. Everyone has different levels of energy and different states of mind at different times and our behaviour always has an impact on others as a result. How people behave and feel is under their own control or influence, but this can be difficult at times. Everyone gets the most from any experience if both energy and attitude are high, but if individuals cannot achieve this then potentially it creates difficulties for the rest of the set membership. This is shown in Figure 11.1.

Figure 11.1 Energy investment model

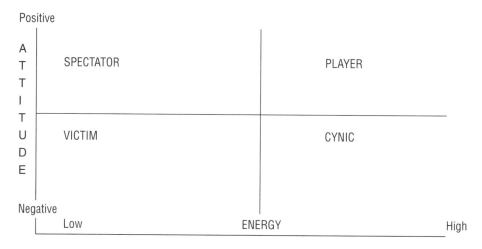

Figure 11.1 shows two dimensions: energy, which can be high or low, and attitude, which can be positive or negative. This creates four cells in the matrix: spectator, victim, cynic and player.

SPECTATORS

Spectators:

- feel positive about what is happening and want to contribute
- are anxious and lacking in confidence
- are reluctant to get involved
- feel threatened when too exposed
- are reluctant to take risks
- are most comfortable when 'watching from the sidelines'.

They tend to react by:

- acknowledging good ideas but being reluctant to change
- working harder than ever at previously successful behaviour
- avoiding taking risks
- trying to 'ride things out' till things return to normal
- keeping a low profile.

The kind of support which spectators need includes:

- understanding and help in coping with fear and a lack of confidence
- effective role models
- plenty of feedback, encouragement and positive reinforcement
- stretching, but achievable challenges.

The kind of questions which will stimulate spectators include:

- 'Why do you think that this might not apply to you?'
- 'Who will do this for you if you don't do it for yourself?'
- 'How could you justify leaving this to others?'
- 'What's stopping you from having a go?'
- 'Can you afford to miss this opportunity?'

VICTIMS

Victims have bruised self-esteem and feel:

- unhappy or depressed
- overwhelmed by work
- powerless and fearful of mistakes.

They tend to react by:

- blocking out challenges
- avoiding confronting issues
- retreating into safety
- avoiding risk and doing the minimum
- avoiding thinking about what might happen.

The support they need includes:

- understanding and help in dealing with stress and frustration
- peer encouragement
- a series of mini-challenges and successes to rebuild their confidence.

Useful questions for victims include:

- 'Do you really want to feel like this?'
- 'How much can you get back in control?'
- 'Who might help you get back in control?'
- 'What could you do to make a start?'
- 'What is the worst thing that could happen if you tried something new?'

CYNICS

Cynics feel:

- not listened to, excluded and constrained
- rebellious and determined to block change which they do not own
- surprised at the stress felt by others
- that they are right, and angry at the world for ignoring them
- frustrated with the confusion and whinging
- overly confident in their own ability.

They tend to react by:

- expressing frustration over the pain and hesitancy of others
- arguing against changes and always seeing the negatives
- pressing for quick solutions and decisive actions, and then criticizing them
- being oblivious to the consequences of their negativity
- bringing both victims and spectators round to their perspective.

The support which cynics need includes:

- humouring – but to a point
- to be given a chance to take personal responsibility
- paring with a player
- confronting about the negative aspects of their behaviour
- reminding what the set and/or the project is all about
- clear boundaries and groundrules set.

Helpful questions for cynics include:

- 'How much do you know about the impact you have on others?'
- 'What happened to make you feel this way?'
- 'Could you see things differently?'
- 'Could you get a better return on your efforts? How?'
- 'Would there be a better time to do this?'

PLAYERS

Players make excellent set members, and typically feel:

- challenged and stretched
- comfortable with the need to change
- open to possibilities and ideas
- optimistic about the longer-term future
- in control of their own destiny
- not afraid of short-term mistakes and setbacks.

They tend to react by:

- seeking the silver-lining beneath the dark clouds
- viewing ambiguity and changes as challenge and opportunity
- finding humour in different situations and using it as a tool
- treating life as a continual learning experience
- expanding their personal comfort zone.

What players need is:

- reward and support for being key people in change and transition
- flexible growth opportunities coupled with visible rewards
- latitude to do it their way and to model effective behaviour to others
- support when they take a stand against a cynic
- respect, recognition and thanks
- not to have a lot of the work of the set dumped on them.

Useful questions for players include:

- 'Are you taking others along with you or are you too far ahead of the pack?'
- 'Might others see you as chameleon-like, or as flip and shallow?'
- 'How sensitive are you to the fear of change in others?'
- 'Is your optimism with regard to the future well founded or not?'

Chapter 12

Dealing with anxiety in action learning

Faced with the choice between changing one's mind and proving that there is no need to do so, almost everybody gets busy on the proof.

(John Kenneth Galbraith)

It is important to remember that what goes on within a set meeting is not just an intellectual or rational process. Set members will all have had previous positive and negative learning experiences (in the education system and in work organizations) that they inevitably view through the spectrum of their personal emotional and psychological history. Those learning experiences will also have been shaped by the processes within those work and social groups of which they have been members and also conditioned by the broader social, economic and political forces operating inside and outside their work organization.

As a result some set members, in common with many adult learners, will face the problem of anxiety, of their ability to cope and of a low level of self-esteem. This can take a number of forms: a fear of disappointing the set adviser as a perceived authority figure, a low self-assessment of abilities and resources or an unwillingness to admit any need at all to others. Typically, such people see the cause of failure as lying in themselves. The manifestations of this anxiety can take a number of forms:

- Fear of failure in the eyes of the set or the set adviser: such people will find difficulty in taking even calculated risks, will tend to undervalue the importance of feelings and are seldom spontaneous in their interactions with others.
- Reluctance to join in: an unwillingness to be playful with ideas and behaviours for fear of appearing foolish – a reluctance to consider 'What if ...?', resulting in highly serious and over-academic behaviour.
- Narrow self-view: a sense of 'resource myopia' – an inability (or unwillingness) to see themselves or others as potential resources to work on the problem; a sense of 'I can't do it, I know I can't!'
- Fear of ambiguity: an avoidance of situations and issues which lack clarity or where the possible outcomes are unknown or not predictable. A reluctance to try something else to see if it works and an over-emphasis on the known at the expense of the unknown.
- Fear of disorder: a dislike of complexity and confusion and a preference for order, balance, and so on, often manifested into a polarization into opposites,

for example, good/bad, right/wrong, and so on and a failure to integrate the best from seemingly opposing viewpoints.

- Fear of influencing others: a concern not to seem pushy or aggressive and so a hesitation in identifying with new, emergent points of view.

Action learning involves working on a problem – a new, challenging and unfamiliar task – and this will carry a degree of risk (of success and failure). Risk, in turn raises these feelings of anxiety, and the tendency for many people (especially in work organizations) is to seek sanctuary in the views of experts who provide anxiety-reducing answers and thus offer what seems like safety and security. Action learning, by contrast, concentrates on helping people to own and focus on their problem, rather than relying on expert advice; it encourages people to develop their own solutions, rather than adopting someone else's, and it emphasizes learning how to learn, through the provision of the action learning set as a facilitating structure. This is shown in Figure 12.1.

Figure 12.1 Alternative means of dealing with anxiety

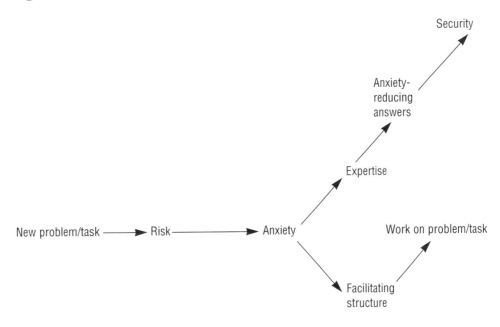

The potential sources of anxiety can include: the set member's work role itself; the particular nature of the problem or task which they bring to the set; ambiguity and uncertainty over the exact nature and purpose of the set itself and of the set member's place within it.

Anxiety in a set member can lead to a number of problem or task 'avoidance behaviours' (Linklater and Kellner, 2000) or 'defensive routines' (Argyris, 1990), which include:

- Treating the set as a therapy group and using it to explore personal issues at the expense of seeking to identify and resolve work problems.
- The set membership starts acting as an agony aunt in an advice-giving session; little real attempt is made to listen actively to the problem-holder in seeking to diagnose their problem.
- Using the set as a 'vicar's tea-party' where nothing more than a pleasant social gathering takes place – a kind of holiday from the rigours of organizational life.
- Portraying one's self to the other set members as a hero (self-idealizing) or a villain (self-deprecating).

Yet the value of the action learning set is that it offers a facilitating or enabling structure which can act as a holding environment or transitional space in which set members' anxiety can be faced, understood and worked-through with the support and challenge of their colleagues and the facilitating set adviser. The set adviser and set members can help to build up the confidence of their 'comrades in adversity' through developing the levels of respect and trust within the set; by modelling the appropriate behaviour to each other and by addressing such matters directly rather than implicitly. It will take time, but it can be done.

No gain without pain.

(Benjamin Franklin)

Chapter 13

The set adviser role: what it involves

The role of the action learning set adviser (or facilitator) effectively comprises two important activities: reading and nudging. Reading involves recognizing the patterns of interaction, activity and interdependence between set members – the informal sub-groupings and alliances; the shared understandings and the differences. Effective reading involves three activities:

1 Taking in from the self: this is the recognition and awareness of what feelings the set adviser is personally experiencing and how they are reacting to them.
2 Taking in from the set: here the set adviser is listening, watching and sensing what is taking place in the set at the level of process – *how* people are saying things to each other.
3 Making sense of it: this involves seeking to distinguish between those immediate and short-term versus those longer-term problems within the group, and what behaviour may be unintended and accidental as against that which might be deliberate. At no time, however, does the set adviser interpret the behaviour of set members; he or she simply describes the patterns they see and asks relevant questions of set members.

Nudging involves the set adviser's interventions in the work of the set. Interventions should be rare, appropriate and with the idea constantly in mind that the purpose of any intervention is to facilitate the learning of a single set member or of the entire group. The set adviser can achieve this by:

• acting as a role model for appropriate behaviour to all set members
• encouraging involvement, initially through the setting of groundrules (for example, on equal airtime)
• ensuring that the setting for set meetings is not subject to external interruptions
• encouraging participation from quieter members
• managing time – starting and stopping times and the airtime of individual set members
• enabling learning, typically through questions which seek to raise set members' awareness and encouraging their reflection and ownership of the problem or issue which confronts them.

In doing this nudging the set adviser serves to foster a sense of collective identity among the set members and emphasizes their mutual interdependence. This is shown in Figure 13.1.

Figure 13.1 Set advising as reading and nudging

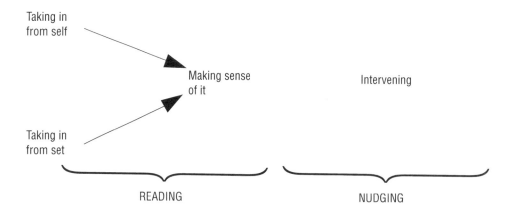

THE SET ADVISER – A FACILITATOR

The set adviser is a facilitator, there to enable the learning process to take place by helping to create the conditions which make it possible for set members to learn from their own experience and that of others while working on their projects (and themselves). The set adviser is *not* there to lead the set, to control it, to chair meetings, nor to provide solutions to problems. The set adviser is 'the guide on the side' and not the 'sage on the stage'. It is inevitable that the set adviser will be most active in the early life of the set, as participants find their feet, get to know each other, agree groundrules, set an agenda, and so on. Thereafter, the interventions of the set adviser need to be:

- judicious – wise and careful
- gentle and tentative
- timely, and above all
- based upon an intention to be helpful and foster learning.

Chapter 14

What makes for competence in set advising?

In order to arrive at what you do not know,
You must go by the way which is the way of ignorance.

(T.S. Eliot, 'The Four Quartets')

There are a number of personal qualities or competencies that a set adviser should display. David Casey (1976) identifies five such qualities:

1 Tolerance of ambiguity: the set adviser lives in a world of uncertainty and must be prepared to allow learners to take control from them. Unless the set adviser welcomes this then he or she will not enjoy the role.
2 Openness and frankness: this is an ability to recognize and express personal feelings in the learning situation, as they arise.
3 Patience: in endless quantities!
4 An overwhelming desire to see people learn: the learning process is likely to happen slowly, incrementally and very personally. So powerful is the desire to speed things up that the set adviser will spend much time 'biting their tongue', not intervening (unless it is helpful) for fear of upsetting the value of the learning process within the set.
5 Empathy, or as Bob Dylan said: 'I wish that for just one time you could stand inside my shoes/And just for that one minute I could be you.' ('Positively 4th Street').

To these qualities Mike Pedler (1996) has added:

• Understanding the micro-politics of the organization: realizing how things get done, where power lies and how it might be mobilized for change.
• The ability to summarize and draw the 'big picture': an ability to pull all the strands together and try to make sense of what has gone on, combined with an awareness of the broader context within which the work of the set and its members takes place.
• The ability to question oneself: the skill to admit personal uncertainties and mistakes in such a way that it does not threaten the security of the set but, rather, shows that the facilitator is human too!

SKILLS NEEDED

From these qualities it is possible to identify the particular skills needed:

- Timing of interventions: too early and the issue is not understood; too late and the opportunity for learning has been lost.
- Asking good questions: which make the problem-holder think, but at the same time feel both supported and challenged, rather than criticized.
- Using the right language: different occupational 'tribes' (managers, professionals, and so on) have different languages (jargon or abbreviations). The rule for the set adviser is 'only connect', so there should be no mystification, no talking down, no falling for the seduction of intellectualizing.
- Choosing issues which help: out of all that might be going on at any one time in the set, the set adviser is able to choose the issue to focus on that links what may be going on in the life of the set with difficulties the problem-holder may be having with the project in their organization.
- Saying nothing and being 'invisible': realizing that to intervene may be to interrupt or short-circuit the learning process of an individual or the whole set membership.
- Parallel-processing: the ability to track a number of processes which are going on in the set at the same time – for most of the time.
- Truthful help: making statements truthfully whilst structuring the statements to be of maximum use to the problem-holder or entire set.

PITFALLS FOR SET ADVISERS

There are a range of pitfalls, each of which might detract substantially from the levels of personal responsibility and involvement required from set members, and which typically stem from the set adviser mistaking their own needs for those of the participants. Chief among these could be the tendency for set members to leave it to the set adviser to notice what is going on and for the set adviser to raise questions, rather than the participants taking that responsibility upon themselves. For example, while discussing a problem-holder's set of options for moving ahead a set member might think 'We've gone over and over this ground before. Why doesn't the set adviser move us on?', rather than saying to the rest of the set 'I keep finding that I'm tuning-out because we've already talked about this before. Are the rest of you still finding this absorbing or not?' Other pitfalls include:

- The expert role: there may be a certain inertia among set advisers to fall back on the expert role which cultivates passivity among set members and a false sense of confidence in the set adviser! This may arise because of the set adviser's perceived skills in understanding (and intervening in) the process of the set.
- The rescuer syndrome: this occurs when a set adviser succumbs to the urge to rescue a set member who is struggling with a particularly difficult issue. The danger is that the set adviser might rescue the participant by throwing them specific suggestions about what they must do to resolve their issue.
- Mistaking the means as the end: it can be very seductive to begin padding the set's process with seemingly small and incremental assignments which, over time, insidiously change the set's process into a traditional learning programme.

For example, in the 'Supporting the process' section there is a discussion on the use of learning diaries. If the set adviser were to unilaterally indicate that this was a requirement of working in the set, set members would complete the learning diaries because they were supposed to rather than because they saw it as something helping their learning, and would be diverted into worrying whether they were recording the right information in the right format. Supporting means, such as learning diaries, should be used only after the idea is presented to the set and the set members carefully consider and decide on its applicability to their situation and needs.

- Satisfaction and complacency: when set advisers think that they are expert then it is likely that they have stopped learning and will not have the openness and ability to question themselves, which is central to what they do.

DEVELOPMENT OF SET ADVISERS

The subject-matter expert who is competent only within a small and well-defined field is typified by the university lecturer who operates in a culture dominated largely by research and publications. This is exactly the opposite of the set adviser or facilitator role in action learning and it is therefore very unlikely (although always possible) that set advisers will develop through this route. The set adviser's role is more about certain personal values than knowledge and skill. Set advisers have to personally believe in the approaches and methods they use, and this belief is based upon their own personal experience and introspection, and upon reflection and dialogue with others.

Those seeking to personally develop as set advisers, or those concerned with developing them in organizations would seek to foster:

- self-knowledge on the part of the individual
- experience of being in, and working with, groups and consciously learning from that experience
- understanding of some theoretical models. These would largely be informed by psychology (group process, roles, norms, stages of group development, and so on) but not specifically, for example, from psychotherapy. The field is broader than that and is modelled on assumptions of health and growth, rather than illness and instability. Moreover, understanding drawn from the arts (literature, poetry, and so on) can be just as useful as that derived from the social sciences (sociology, anthropology, economics).

Yet it is ultimately only by actually facilitating an action learning set that a set adviser can really learn how to do it, what it really feels like, and whether they like the experience. This suggests, therefore, that:

- future set advisers might well be drawn from the ranks of earlier participants in action learning sets, as the insights drawn from being a set member can be a vital element in the development of the facilitator role
- if there is to be any formalized facilitator training then, as well as developing an understanding of appropriate theory, it should also provide an opportunity for practice in facilitation of groups, for feedback on performance and opportunity to reflect on this
- perhaps using the set approach itself is likely to produce the best results. This would involve creating a set of set advisers whose problem or project would be

their own facilitation of their own sets. They would meet on an agreed basis in a set with their own facilitator and use the action learning approach to develop their competence, thus modelling the behaviour and 'taking their own medicine'.

Chapter 15

Key questions in action learning

The real object of education is to have a man in the condition
Of constantly asking questions.

(Bishop Creighton)

Earlier review of the process of action learning sets identified questioning as a
major element of the challenge which, together with security and support, are the
stimulus to the development of questioning insight. Experience with action
learning sets has also identified a range of specific useful questions which can
serve to help problem-holders address their project or issue.

THE THREE KEY QUESTIONS

Revans originally identified three major questions related to addressing the
problem or project:

1 *Who knows ... about the problem?* Who has useful information? Hard facts
   which will determine the dimensions of the problem, not opinions, views, half-
   truths or official policies.
2 *Who cares ... about the problem?* Who has the emotional investment in getting
   change made? Who is involved in and committed to the outcome, not who
   talks about the problem?
3 *Who can ... do anything about the problem?* Who has the power to reorder
   resources so that changes can occur? Who, when faced with facts, commitment
   and energy, has the power to say 'Yes'?

The questions refer, of course, to the three crucial processes in human action –
thinking, feeling and willing. Most of our formal education has concentrated only
on the first question and the thinking process. Yet, how much emotional
commitment (feeling) and power (willing) exists are important. If solutions are
based solely on such left-brain thinking there is a danger of 'paralysis by analysis'
where diagnosis and planning never leads to action.

QUESTIONS FOR PROBLEM-HOLDERS

There are other helpful questions which each problem-holder, in preparing for their slot in the progress-reporting part of a set meeting, can ask themselves:

- What am I trying to do?
- What's stopping me from doing it?
- How do I feel about that?
- What can I do about it?
- Who knows what I am trying to do? Who has the necessary information?
- Who cares about what I am trying to do? Who feels emotionally involved?
- Who can do anything to help? Who has the 'clout' to make a difference?
- What has happened since the last set meeting?
- What has been different from what I expected?
- What did I not do and why?
- What did I do instead and why?
- What would a positive outcome look like?
- What have I (or can I) learn from this?

QUESTIONS FOR SET MEMBERS AND SET ADVISERS

Similarly, there are a number of questions which the other set members and the set adviser might want to use to help the problem-holder, including:

- What do you want to get out of your slot?
- Can you give us a blow-by-blow account of things as they happened?
- What have you (or can you) learn from that?
- What do you most need from us (the set) now?
- How do other people involved in this (colleagues, bosses, staff, partner, friends, and so on) feel about this?
- What are your feelings about what's happening?
- What questions does that raise for you?
- How can we help you get some movement on this issue?
- How might somcone you admire deal with this problem?
- Can you think of three action possibilities?
- What are the pros and cons of these possibilities?
- What are the first action steps you intend to take before the next set meeting?

Likewise, the set adviser (or in well-functioning and mature sets, also set members) could well ask:

- Can we just stop for a second and check on how we're doing?
- How do you feel about what's going on?
- How helpful was that comment?
- Would you be able to turn that comment into a question?
- What questions does that raise for you?
- What question was the most helpful?
- Who or what is helping you most at the moment in the set?
- Why did everyone ignore what Bill said?
- There seems to be a lack of energy at the moment. Should we take a break?
- Maybe we should go back to our groundrules and check them again?
- What exactly are we trying to do here?

- How might we be able to help Audrey move forward on this?
- What I think I heard Jim say was ...
- How might we make this set more effective?
- What does that really mean?
- Why is that important?
- When you say 'we' do you mean 'me'?
- Am I being helpful?

Live the questions now!

(Rainer Maria Rilke)

Chapter 16

Supporting the process: diagnostics, reflecting on practice and planning action

The real voyage of discovery consists not in seeking new lands, but with seeing with new eyes.

(Marcel Proust)

On page 52 I introduced the danger of mistaking means for ends when seeking to support the learning process in action learning sets. This part of the toolkit contains material which can help set members:

- diagnose the development and learning climate in their organization (or their part of the organization) and consider the influence of their personal learning styles
- reflect on their personal practice, whether managerial or professional
- plan action to further their learning and activity in their organization.

USING SUPPORT MATERIAL

This material should be used with great care, as it may confuse ends with means and the classical situation of the tail wagging the dog may develop. Such material should only be used, therefore, when:

- it has been presented and described to the membership of the set by the set adviser
- set participants have had adequate time and opportunity to consider the pros and cons of using the material
- individual set members and the set as a whole make a definite decision.

The reason that support material may be helpful is due to the innate and overwhelming seductiveness of the task or problem – an obsession by set members with action at the expense of learning. The support material can serve to divert people away from the task and towards learning about the processes by which the task is achieved, and so emphasize the importance of learning objectives alongside task objectives. It forces explicit discussion within the set of learning processes and achievements both in the workplace (out there) and among the set members (in here).

> Now we see through a glass darkly, but then we shall see face to face;
> Now I know in part; then I shall understand fully.
>
> (1 Corinthians, 13:12)

DIAGNOSTICS

Three possible diagnostic tools are considered here:

1 The workplace development climate questionnaire.
2 The learning climate questionnaire.
3 Questionnaires on individual learning styles.

WORKPLACE DEVELOPMENT CLIMATE QUESTIONNAIRE

This questionnaire helps people to analyse the climate in their organization (or their part of the organization) in relation to the development of staff.

Introduction

Here are some statements about some aspects of your present work organization and your experience of it. Please read each statement carefully and decide whether you agree or disagree with the statement in terms of your own work experience and employing organization. Then place a cross in the appropriate box alongside.

There are no right or wrong answers and this is not a test of ability or intelligence. So work steadily through it, and please be frank.

	Agree	Disagree
1 Everyone in the organization generally knows what contribution he or she makes to the whole.		
2 Management are not very approachable.		
3 Loyalty to one's own department or profession tends to come first.		
4 Everyone is pleased when the organization is successful.		

5 People spend a lot of time blaming others for their mistakes. ☐ ☐

6 I generally know where to go when I want help. ☐ ☐

7 They tell us we are here to carry out instructions. ☐ ☐

8 I am proud of the success of my organization. ☐ ☐

9 Decisions always seem to come down from the top. ☐ ☐

10 There seems to be quite a lot of friction and not much co-operation between departments and professions. ☐ ☐

11 Management encourages bosses to discuss new proposals with their staff. ☐ ☐

12 People normally consider the effect of their actions upon the whole organization. ☐ ☐

13 The only way we learn of changes is by the grapevine. ☐ ☐

14 It is not uncommon here to get conflicting instructions and orders. ☐ ☐

15 On the whole, people do not feel very free to speak their minds. ☐ ☐

16 People seem to prefer to get on with the job by themselves. ☐ ☐

17 One's job depends not so much on titles or activities, but on what sort of position you can carve out for yourself. ☐ ☐

18 Normally staff are expected to accept direction without question. ☐ ☐

19 People in the organization only get together when there is a crisis. ☐ ☐

20 Managers place value on the opinions of staff. ☐ ☐

21 In my job I am rather unclear about what goes on in other functions, departments or professions. ☐ ☐

22 I don't think many people below senior management really understand the organization's objectives. ☐ ☐

23 I often find it difficult to know who to approach for information. ☐ ☐

24 Managers seem more concerned with the narrow interest of their function, department or profession rather than wider organizational objectives. ☐ ☐

25 Management is pretty intolerant of error and is not very good at listening to explanations. ☐ ☐

26 On the whole, communication in the organization seems to be pretty full and free. ☐ ☐

27 In our organization, staff are not afraid to say what they think. ☐ ☐

28 Wider involvement in management is seen as a desirable objective by the organization. ☐ ☐

29 All too often no one knows what his or her counterpart in another part of the organization is doing about things that affect them both. ☐ ☐

30 Managers tend to use their power to coerce staff. ☐ ☐

31 In our organization, I think staff exercise quite a lot of influence on their bosses. ☐ ☐

32 Most people feel pretty good about the organization. ☐ ☐

33 Management is pretty good at discussing its proposals with staff. ☐ ☐

34 Staff do not seem very involved in decisions related to their work. ☐ ☐

35 It is only by experience that you get to know the right people to go to. ☐ ☐

36 Bosses seem to keep changing their minds without consultation. ☐ ☐

37 Better results, it is felt, are obtained by involving everyone in the problems. ☐ ☐

38 The general direction of communications seems to be downwards. ☐ ☐

39 Teamwork is a feature of everyday life. ☐ ☐

40 There seems to be a lot of information and voluntary
    co-operation amongst people in our organization.

☐ ☐

41 You're not paid to think in our organization.

☐ ☐

Scoring

Check back on your answer to each question and then refer to the score key
which follows. You need to set up two vertical columns on a separate piece of
paper headed 'I' (for integrated) and 'P' (for permissive) respectively. The
numbers on the score key should then be transferred to the appropriate column.
For example, if you have agreed with question 1 you score 2 under your 'I'
column. If you disagree, you score 0. If for question 4 you have agreed, you score
1 under the 'I' column and 1 under the 'P' column. If you have disagreed with
question 4 you score 0.

When the totals under your 'I' and 'P' columns are added up (they should come
to no more than 32) they should be entered into the boxes below

☐ I (Integrated)

☐ P (Permissive)

and then plotted as a single point (rather like plotting a map reference) in the
matrix below the scoring key. They will fall into one of four cells in the matrix:
autocratic/integrated, integrated/permissive, autocratic/fragmented and
fragmented/permissive (see page 65 for descriptions).

Scoring key

QUESTION NO.	SCORE IF YOU AGREE	SCORE IF YOU DISAGREE
One	2 (I)	—
Two	—	1 (P)
Three	—	1 (I)
Four	1 (P), 1 (I)	—
Five	—	1 (I)
Six	1 (I)	—
Seven	—	2 (P)
Eight	2 (P)	—
Nine	—	1 (P)
Ten	—	2 (I)
Eleven	2 (P)	—
Twelve	1 (I)	—
Thirteen	—	1 (P), 1 (I)
Fourteen	—	2 (I)
Fifteen	—	1 (P)
Sixteen	—	1 (I)
Seventeen	—	1 (I)
Eighteen	—	2 (P)
Nineteen	—	1 (I)
Twenty	2 (P)	—
Twenty-one	—	2 (I)
Twenty-two	—	1 (P), 1 (I)
Twenty-three	—	1 (I)
Twenty-four	—	2 (I)
Twenty-five	—	1 (P)
Twenty-six	1 (P), 1 (I)	—
Twenty-seven	1 (P), 1 (I)	—
Twenty-eight	2 (P)	—
Twenty-nine	—	2 (I)
Thirty	—	1 (P)
Thirty-one	1 (P)	—
Thirty-two	1 (P), 1 (I)	—
Thirty-three	2 (P)	—
Thirty-four	—	1 (P)
Thirty-five	—	1 (I)
Thirty-six	—	1 (P), 1 (I)
Thirty-seven	1 (P)	—
Thirty-eight	—	1 (P)
Thirty-nine	2 (I)	—
Forty	1 (P), 1 (I)	—
Forty-one	—	1 (P)

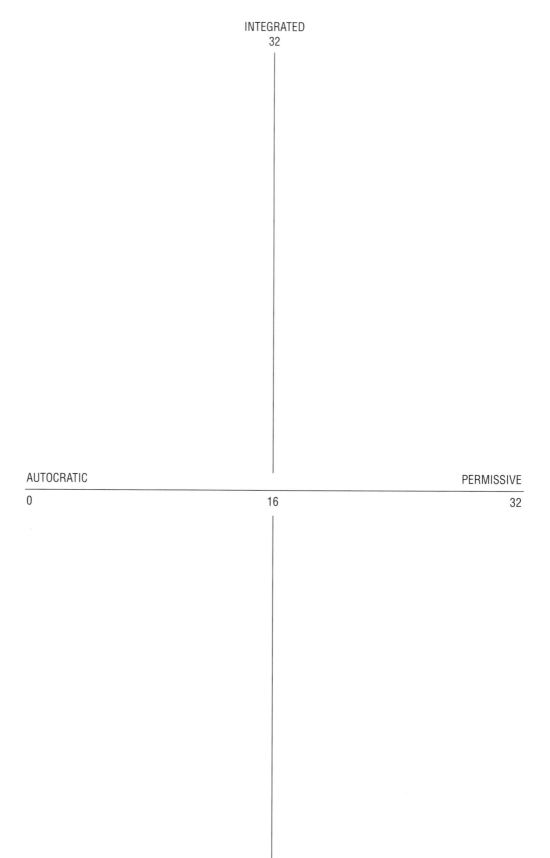

INTEGRATED
32

AUTOCRATIC   PERMISSIVE

0   16   32

0
FRAGMENTED

THE ACTION LEARNER'S TOOLKIT

The matrix is based upon two dimensions – autocratic/permissive (P) and fragmented/integrated (I) and creates four cells.

In the fragmented-permissive cell there is general support for individual and organizational development, but this is bitty – not focused or co-ordinated in any real way. The organization may be prone to initiative-itis with a number of developmental hares being set running at once. Targeting of resources for development is poor and may be based on the principle of 'blue-eyed boys and girls'.

In the autocratic-fragmented cell there will be a clear sense of organizational direction, set from the top in a hierarchical fashion. Developmental activity may not be seen as contributing to that sense of direction or, if it is seen as a contributing factor, there is likely to be little or no cohesion or rationale to it.

There is also a clear top-led command-and-control sense of organizational direction in the autocratic-integrated cell, which typically operates with a single dominant world view and power centre. *All* developmental activity which exists is required to conform to bolstering and furthering this perspective and direction and little deviant or leading-edge approaches will be tolerated (too risky!).

Finally, in the integrated-permissive cell there is an overall broad sense of direction, but recognition that there may well be a variety of routes in getting there. Diversity or freedom within a framework is valued and a degree of controlled experimentation in development terms is seen as useful insurance against an uncertain future.

LEARNING CLIMATE QUESTIONNAIRE

This questionnaire was devised by Mike Pedler and Tom Boydell (Pedler and Boydell, 1999). Its purpose is to help the individual learner to diagnose how well the culture in their organization supports learning.

For each of the following questions, ring the number that you think best represents the quality of the learning climate in your organization. 1 is very poor and 7 is excellent.

1 Physical environment
The amount and quality of space and privacy afforded to people; the temperature, noise, ventilation and comfort levels.

People are cramped
with little privacy and poor
conditions

People have plenty of space
and good surroundings
surroundings

1	2	3	4	5	6	7

2 Learning resources
Numbers, quality and availability of training and development staff and resources (books, CD-Roms, videos, films, training packages, equipment, etc.).

Very few or no trained
people; poor resources and
equipment

Many development
people and lots of
resources; very good
facilities

1	2	3	4	5	6	7

3 Encouragement to learn
The extent to which people feel encouraged to have ideas, take risks, experiment and learn new ways of doing old tasks.

Little encouragement
to learn; low expectations
of people in terms of new
skills and abilities

People are encouraged
to learn at all times and to
extend themselves and
their knowledge

1	2	3	4	5	6	7

4 Communications
How open and free is the flow of information? Do people express ideas and opinions easily and openly?

Feelings kept to self;
secretive; information
is hoarded

People are usually
ready to give their
views and pass on
information

1	2	3	4	5	6	7

5 Rewards

How well rewarded are people for effort? Is recognition given for good work or are people punished and blamed?

People are ignored
but then blamed when
things go wrong

People are recognized
for good work and rewarded
for effort and learning

1	2	3	4	5	6	7

6 Conformity

The extent to which people are expected to conform to rules, norms, regulations and policies, rather than think.

There is conformity
to rules and standards at
all times – no personal
responsibility taken or
given

People manage themselves
and do their work as they see
fit; great emphasis on taking
personal responsibility

1	2	3	4	5	6	7

7 Value placed on ideas

How much are ideas, opinions and suggestions sought out, encouraged and valued?

People are not paid
to think; their ideas
are not valued

Efforts are made to get
people to put ideas
forward; there is a view
that the future rests on
people's ideas

1	2	3	4	5	6	7

8 Practical help available

The extent to which people help each other, lend a hand, offer skills, knowledge or support.

People do not help each
other; there is unwillingness
to pool or share resources

People very willing and
helpful; pleasure is
taken in the success
of others

1	2	3	4	5	6	7

9 Warmth and support

How friendly are people in the organization? Do people support, trust and like one another?

Little warmth and support;
this is a cold isolation

Warm and friendly place;
people enjoy coming to
work

1	2	3	4	5	6	7

10 Standards

The emphasis placed upon quality in all things; people set challenging standards for themselves and each other.

Low standards and quality; no one really gives a damn				High standards; everyone cares and people pick each other up on work quality		
1	2	3	4	5	6	7

11 Learning leadership

How the organization's leaders inspire learning.

Managers never discuss their own learning				Managers openly and frequently share their learning experiences		
1	2	3	4	5	6	7

12 Personal learning plans

How personal learning objectives are supported.

Individuals do not record their own learning objectives				Personal learning plans are recorded and regularly reviewed		
1	2	3	4	5	6	7

To evaluate the learning climate of your organization, add the total of all the numbers you ringed. If your score comes to 35 or less you are working in a poor learning climate. You will be able to identify the areas that need attention by examining the low scoring questions. *A learning organization aspires to score more than 55.*

If you would like to improve the strength of the learning climate in your workplace, look back over the questions where you scored less than 4. These are the areas you should focus on.

Source: Pedler and Boydell (1999). Material reproduced with the kind permission of Lemos & Crane, London.

QUESTIONNAIRES ON INDIVIDUAL LEARNING STYLES

A number of questionnaires also exist to help individuals assess their own personal learning style. The original work in this sphere was undertaken by David Kolb (Kolb, 1984) and his ideas, for example on learning and problem-solving, clearly underlie action learning. The self-diagnostic method which he devised – the learning style inventory (LSI) – has, however, been criticized for being culture-bound and has found less favour as time has passed. Instead, the learning style questionnaire (LSQ), created by Peter Honey and Alan Mumford (1995), has proved more popular. This identifies four styles:

1 Activist: who thrives on learning from challenges and new experiences.
2 Reflector: who tends to be cautious, standing back and observing experiences from different perspectives.
3 Theorist: who adapts and integrates observations into logically sound theories.
4 Pragmatist: who likes to try out new ideas, theories and techniques to see if they work in practice.

Honey and Mumford argue that everyone develops their own characteristic profile across these four styles, although they also point out:

• A person's learning style is not fixed and is capable of change – and, indeed, does frequently change in response to a variety of external influences and situations.
• The information which people gain from the results of the LSQ should not be used to avoid particular types of learning but should instead provide a basis for developing a learning approach which results in a more balanced profile.

Further details about the LSQ can be obtained from:

Peter Honey Publications Ltd
10 Linden Avenue
MAIDENHEAD
Berkshire
SL6 6HB
UK
Tel: 01628 633946
Fax: 01628 633262
Email: orders@peterhoney.com
Web: www.peterhoney.com

There is, however, a danger of using the LSQ (or the LSI or any other assessment tool) as a typology – dividing people into discrete categories. When people pin labels on themselves ('I'm a reflector') they might believe that, once they have identified their learning style, this is a fixed personality trait which cannot be changed. As a result they must learn to work within their limitations, seeking only experiences which require their preferred style and avoiding those which offer a different approach. This can also be reinforced by the behaviour of facilitators who might foster the idea that people are only really capable of learning in one particular way.

Such a view is clearly not what Honey and Mumford intended and runs counter to the thinking about adult learning which underpins action learning. Used with care and sensitivity, however, the LSQ and other diagnostics can support action learning, with the never-to-be-forgotten rider that they must never be mistaken for ends – they are only means to help and stimulate the learning process.

REFLECTING ON PRACTICE

> The only person who is educated is the one who has learned how to learn and change.
>
> (Carl Rogers)

In the sphere of professional work (teachers, nurses, doctors, and so on) the notion that professional practice is best improved by structured reflection is a common one, but is less well developed in the managerial sphere. Three useful approaches which help learners to reflect upon what they do are provided here. They are critical incident analysis, learning diaries and biography work. All are, in slightly different ways, based on the reflective cycle model shown in Figure 16.1.

Figure 16.1 Reflective cycle model

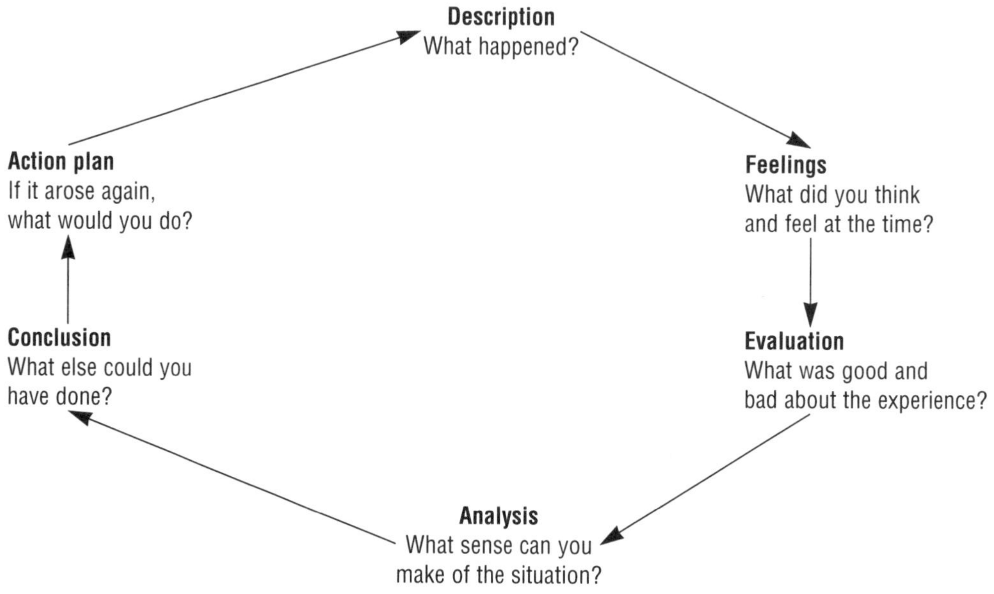

Adapted from Gibbs (1988).

CRITICAL INCIDENT ANALYSIS

This is an approach which is used to elicit those aspects of a job, or what people do, which are critical to success or failure and to find out what behaviours are critical to good or poor job performance. The emphasis is on the process – *how* people behave in successful or unsuccessful ways. Critical incident analysis typically involves a number of stages:

• Describing a significant recent (within the last 12 months) incident which did or did not meet a goal or objective, or in which the person felt they were particularly effective or ineffective. This could just as easily be something accomplished which was ordinary as something which was extraordinary. The more vivid the description of the incident the better. In effect it is a narrative account, in chronological order, of the events and processes in the situation – what happened, what the person felt, thought and did.
• Reviewing what the person actually did which was effective or ineffective. This could involve:

  – asking what else might have happened, or what else should have happened

- trying to see what happened from another viewpoint
- asking what did not happen and why
- considering what really was the cause of the problem
- considering a reversal of the situation described
- considering what has been left out of the narrative
- asking what personal beliefs, values and assumptions underlie the incident
- asking what were the dilemmas and choices in the situation and why particular choices were made
- asking what needs further consideration and what can be learned from the situation.

It is clear that the processes used in critical incident analysis resonate with the processes of action learning. There are two possible ways in which it might be used to support action learning. First, it could form the basis of the progress-reporting element of set meetings, with the problem-holder offering the narrative and the set members addressing the areas mentioned above. Alternatively, individual set members could use it privately to prepare for a set meeting. Addressing the questions above would provide a helpful checklist and enrich the account of their work on the problem or issue.

LEARNING DIARIES

The purpose of a learning diary (or learning log) is twofold: to record the experience of a set member during the set meetings, and to make connections between the set meeting experience and experience back in the workplace, including attempts to move the project forward. This is done in order to encourage and develop the process of reflection on personal learning and development.

In offering the idea of learning diaries for set members the set adviser would follow the suggestions made above, that is, present the idea and let set members decide individually or collectively whether it would be a useful thing to do or not. Paradoxically, those who might benefit most from the reflective processes embodied in learning diaries are often those (such as people with a high activist profile in the learning styles questionnaire) who are most likely to resist using this approach! If they do decide to use the approach then the set adviser might helpfully suggest that:

- set members should be frank and sincere in what they write
- rather than a single prescribed format, they might like to use a variety of means – drawings, cartoons, quotable quotes, newspaper cuttings, and so on – if they can aid the reflective process
- a degree of self-discipline is needed to find the time and space to write-up the learning diary on a regular basis.

A useful learning diary is one which is both sequential and reflective. The sequential element involves jotting down notes on a continuing and regular basis under such headings as:

- People: those in the set or in work situations who have an effect on the set member – their physical appearance and behaviours, verbal and non-verbal.
- Events: key or potent activities and incidents that take place at work or in a set meeting.

- Reactions: what the set member thought, felt, wanted and did – whatever was strong enough to be noticeable.
- Insights: capturing ideas or thoughts that particularly impressed or influenced the set member – either their own conclusions or other people's that were heard.
- Learning: based on the reactions and insights, what greater sense can the set member make of what is happening to them and others?

The reflective aspect could involve the participant asking themselves the following questions at various points across the action learning programme:

- Planning: What did I plan to do?
  How did I prepare myself?
- Action: What happened?
  What have I achieved and why?
  What haven't I achieved and why?
  Was it what I anticipated?
  If yes, what went well?
  If no, what could I have done differently?
- Review: How did I spend my time?
  Did I do what I planned?
  If not, what stopped me?
  How effective was my self-management?
  Has my thinking changed and, if so, how?
  Have my feelings changed and, if so, how?
  Have my actions changed and, if so, how?
  What have I learned?
  How did I learn it?
- Planning: What do I want to do more of in future?
  How will I go about it?
  What do I want to do less of in future?
  How will I go about it?
  What do I want to do differently in future?
  How will I go about it?
  How do I feel about this?

Review of learning diaries can provide set members with material to bring to the progress-reporting part of the set meeting and there could also be a role for them as personal source material for evaluation of action learning programmes (see below).

BIOGRAPHY WORK

The scope of action learning, drawing from the body of evidence of how adults learn, extends wider than a single job, a single problem or a single organization. Its concern with how individuals make sense of the situations they find themselves in means that the focus extends to the individual's career path and indeed their complete life cycle, for making personal choices is shaped by a whole range of different influences, not just organizational or occupational ones.

Thus what is loosely described as biography work can also be a possible support to the learning processes of programme participants. It offers a way for individuals to review their existence in ways which transcend the narrow, ahistorical snapshots that many analytical approaches embody and which produces an enriched perspective which brings the past and possible futures together with the present for the purposes of understanding and action. As such it has been used to support people seeking to place job or career problems in a life context (Forrester and Webb, 1992).

Two examples are offered here: the life goals exercise and the core process exercise.

Life goals exercise

This exercise is drawn from the work of Herbert Shepard on Life and Career Planning (French and Bell, 1999).

Draw an individual lifeline as shown in Figure 16.2, where one dimension is the passage of time from the individual's birth and the other relates to feelings of self-esteem, ranging from high to low.

Figure 16.2 Drawing a lifeline

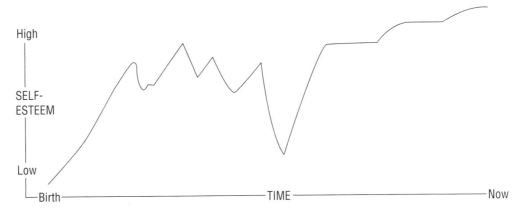

Prepare a life inventory of important personal 'happenings', including:

- any peak experiences
- things which you do well
- things which you do poorly
- things you would like to stop doing
- things you would like to learn to do well
- peak experiences you would like to have
- values you want to live
- things you would like to start doing now.

Take 20 minutes to write your obituary.

Core Process Exercise (Jones, 1992)

- Divide your life into four or five sections, from birth to the present day.
- Recall those moments, feelings, sensations and experiences which were fulfilling and motivating – the times of feeling at one with oneself and the world.
- Identify the special qualities, important patterns and themes which were around at the time of these moments.

Biography approaches tend to be highly meaningful for people who are in mid-career, who are contemplating a career or life change or who have seldom been introspective about their own lifestyle and career pattern. It should be entirely voluntary whether participants opt to undertake such work, and the earlier caveats about means and ends apply here too.

PLANNING ACTION

No one knows what he can do until he tries.

(Publilius Syrus, *c.* 442 BC)

If the work of action learning sets is to be more than navel contemplation then effective linkage to the organization, the work setting and the problem location is necessary. The actions which the set member will plan to take may include some related to the individual's own personal development, while others will deal with actions taken in conjunction with others. Some things may happen quickly, while others may take more time. Although the processes of questioning addressed earlier in this toolkit will help, action learning programme participants will need to develop realistic and robust action plans to ensure that the linkages are made. The more effective the action planning process, the more likely real change will happen. Clear action planning should also aid the evaluation of action learning (see below).

An action plan is simply a list of major and minor activities which must be carried out in order to move from where things stand now to some desired future state. An effective action plan is:

- focused on that desired future state of affairs
- specific, with clearly defined activities
- integrated, with the different aspects of the plan being connected together into a whole
- time-sequenced, with a logical chronology of events
- adaptable, with the unexpected anticipated wherever possible and contingencies planned for
- realistic and achievable.

In thinking about what actions might need to be taken the notion of 'early wins' or actions which are urgent, but not complex in their implementation, can be helpful, as shown in Figure 16.3.

Figure 16.3 Locating early win actions

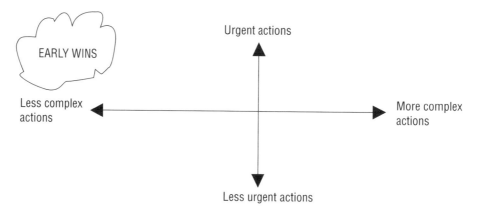

A good action plan will quite simply provide the answers to the questions:

- WHAT needs to happen?
- By WHEN does it need to happen?
- WHO needs to make it happen?

> We must be the change we wish to see in the world.
>
> (Mahatma Gandhi)

Chapter 17

Evaluating action learning

Only those who will risk going too far
Can possibly find out how far one can go.

(T.S. Eliot)

The benefits claimed for action learning are both at the level of the individual (their performance and their personal development) and at the level of organizational capacity and capability.

INDIVIDUAL BENEFITS

At the individual level, action learning claims to provide real opportunities for personal learning and growth. The participants in sets face real issues and problems which they own, and are committed to making progress on them. Thus they need to reflect on how their actions, personal style, values and motivations make an impact on others. The set's focus on action and review helps individuals to experiment and try out different approaches, thereby enhancing their self-awareness.

ORGANIZATIONAL BENEFITS

At the level of the organization (or organizations) action learning claims that benefits include better motivated and more competent individuals, together with:

- a cadre of people familiar with action learning and who can promote the approach to others
- people who share a better understanding of the roles of others in the organization (or in partner organizations) and how they interact
- people who are likely to take more responsibility for the organization as a whole because they have addressed real issues together
- action and progress on problems.

Yet few attempts seem to have been made to evaluate action learning beyond the changes in the behaviour of participants in programmes as perceived directly by the participants themselves, the set advisers, and the immediate programme sponsors or clients. One large-scale impact evaluation (Weiland and Leigh, 1971) concluded that action learning had made a major impact on some individuals, but had made little overall impact on the organization.

There is a growing demand that development activity such as action learning programmes seek to provide some evidence of the return on the investment made by the organization which sets them up. This section of the toolkit seeks to address this problem and to suggest some possible ways forward.

TYPES OF EVALUATION

The first need is to distinguish between different types of evaluation. Some evaluation is formative (or developmental). It is concerned with steering and improving the programme and the activities within it while it is happening. Other evaluation is summative (or judgemental) and is concerned with assessing the impact or contribution of the development activity – whether goals were met and resources well used and the general worthwhileness of the initiative. Formative evaluation should be part of the ongoing activity within each action learning set meeting, and two resources are offered as an aid to this at the end of this section – the set meeting review worksheet (Pedler, 1996) and behaviours in effective learning groups rating scale (Mumford, 1996). However, it is summative evaluation which urgently needs to be addressed. Such evaluation can take place at the level of the individual, the set and the programme or organization as a whole.

At the level of the individual the concern will be to assess progress in working on the problem which the person brought with them, how they have progressed or resolved it and the personal learning which they have derived from the process. Useful questions which can be asked include:

- Has the person changed as a result of involvement in the action learning programme, and if so, how?
- Has the individual developed the individual micro-political skills necessary to get things done in organizations on a continuing basis?

The collection of information to answer these questions can be done by a variety of means, including:

- self-reporting: by asking participants to write a reflective account close to the end of the programme which would focus on both project achievement and individual learning, addressing such questions as 'What have I gained/learned from the programme, or done differently as a result of my involvement – for myself? – for my colleagues and staff in the organization?' If, as part of the programme, participants have been keeping a learning diary, then this would provide a rich source of material for such self-reporting
- questionnaires: to participants and a sample of their staff, bosses and colleagues
- interviews: on a one-to-one basis with a sample of participants, set advisers, bosses, staff and colleagues.

At the level of the set the focus will be on the collective group achievement and on the development and maturity of the set as a group. The key question to be addressed here is 'Has the person been changed by the process of support and challenge taking place in the set?' The data collection methods mentioned above could require answers to this question.

Finally, at the level of the organization, the concern is to assess activity and achievement across the sets and the impact on the organization (or organizations) as a whole. Among the questions which will need to be asked at this level are 'What evidence is there that *real* problems were addressed?' – that is, as opposed to puzzles or contrived problems. The answer to this question may reveal deeper or wider organizational issues than the action learning programme alone can engage with. Another important question will be 'What evidence is there of the ideas and initiatives developed within the sets being tested in action?' Are there individual, group, departmental, professional, age or gender blockages which have been revealed by attempts to implement action from the projects?

At this level too, it will be important to assess the action learning programme as a whole, in terms of effort, process and performance (Raelin, 2000).

In terms of effort:

- What was the cost of the action learning programme?
- How many people participated?
- How much time did it take (for example, in terms of participants being away from their job)?
- Who sponsored the programme and what were their expectations?

In terms of process:

- What need was the action learning programme responding to?
- How were the presenting problem or problems addressed?
- What were the distinguishing features of the programme and how (if at all) should they be changed for any future programmes?
- Which projects were chosen, why and how?
- How were sets put together?

In terms of performance, this can be addressed on both a short-term and long-term basis.

In the short term:

- Were any particular competencies addressed, changed or added?
- What were the participants' reactions to the experience?
- How did other stakeholders, such as the participants' sponsors, react to the experience?
- Was the programme contained within its cost and time parameters?
- Did the projects produce direct beneficial changes?
- Was the need that inspired the programme met?
- How were the sets received?

In the longer term:

- Have programme participants changed their behaviour? Did it result in a salutary effect on their team, department, unit, and so on?
- Was there significant transformation in the participants' personal development, values and practices?
- Did the programme lead to career change or advancement for any participants?
- Have there been any non-intended effects of the programme in other parts of the organization?
- Did the programme promote questioning insight not only in participants, but in those parts of the organization from which they came?

- Has the action learning programme evolved into a significant venture for the organization?
- Did the programme change any cultural norms or organizational practices?
- Were any changes noted in terms of bottom-line results?

PROBLEMS WITH EVALUATION

In seeking to evaluate action learning programmes (as with other developmental activity) it is relatively easy to collect data on reactions (thoughts and feelings about the programme); slightly more difficult, but not impossible to collect data on learning (the knowledge, skills and attitudes acquired or changed by the programme); more problematic (but not impossible) to collect data on changes in job performance behaviour resulting from the programme, and very difficult to collect data on outcomes (the impact or effect of that changed behaviour on organizational performance). The move from reactions to outcomes also introduces a significant number of intervening variables (or other things going on in the organization) and the more difficult it is to ascribe simple and direct cause-and-effect relationships which prove that action learning (or any other approach) is more or less successful.

SET MEETING REVIEW WORKSHEET

Each person should spend 5 minutes reflecting individually on the work of the set, before sharing the results with fellow set members.

My problem: The 3 key things I have learned about my problem today are:

_____

_____

_____

Myself: The one thing I've learned about myself today is:

_____

_____

_____

Action: My action steps before the next meeting are:

_____

_____

_____

_____

_____

_____

Other set members: The most interesting thing I have learned today about the problems facing each of the other set members is:

Name:
_____

_____

_____

Name:
_____

_____

_____

Name:
_____

_____

_____

Name:
_____

_____

_____

Name:
_____

_____

_____

Name:
_____

_____

_____

The set: The thing that stands out for me today in terms of the working of this set is:-

_____
_____
_____
_____
_____
_____

Source: Pedler (1996). The material is reproduced with the kind permission of Lemos & Crane, London.

BEHAVIOURS IN EFFECTIVE LEARNING GROUPS RATING SCALE

Below is a list of the kinds of behaviours which facilitate learning in action learning sets:

- Enabling other set members to share airtime appropriately.
- Being non-defensive about own actions and learning.
- Being supportive about the issues and concerns of fellow set members.
- Being open in initiating and responding to issues.
- Being analytical with regard to own and others' problems.
- Listening actively and with empathy.
- Questioning effectively, in ways which help fellow learners.
- Accepting help from others – in the set and beyond.
- Being creative in response to problems.
- Being innovative in recognizing the learning that can be derived from working on the task or problem.
- Taking appropriate risks.
- Using both the task *and* learning cycles.
- Using the strengths of others as learners to assist self.
- Helping to motivate other set members as learners.

Individually review this list and score each item on a scale from 0 = low, to 10 = high, in terms of the following:

- How effective is my own contribution for each of these statements?
- How effective do I judge the set as a whole to be for each of these contributions?
- What action might I take to improve my own contribution?
- What action might the set take to improve itself?

Source: Mumford (1996).

Bibliography and further reading

Ainslie, M. and Wills, G. (1997), 'Designing a quality action learning process for managers', *Journal of Workplace Learning*, **9** (3), pp. 100–110.

Anthony, W. (1981), 'Using internships for action learning', *Journal of European Industrial Training*, **5** (1), pp. 24–27.

Argyris, C. (1990), *Overcoming Organizational Defences: Facilitating Organizational Learning*, Needham, MA: Allyn & Bacon.

Baird, L., Holland, P. and Deacon, S. (1999), 'Learning from action: imbedding more learning into the performance fast enough to make a difference', *Organizational Dynamics*, **27** (4), pp. 19–32.

Beaty, L., Bourner, T. and Frost, P. (1993), 'Action learning: reflections on becoming a set member', *Management Education and Development*, **24** (4), pp. 350–67.

Boddy, D. (1979), 'Some lessons from an action learning programme', *Journal of European Industrial Training*, **3** (3).

Boddy, D. (1980), 'An action learning programme for supervisors', *Human Resources Development*, **4** (3).

Boddy, D. (1981), 'Putting action learning into action', *Journal of European Industrial Training*, **5** (5), pp. 37–56.

Boisot, M. (1987), 'Chinese boxes and learning cubes: action learning in a cross-cultural context', *Journal of Management Development*, **6** (2).

Bourner, T. (1996), 'What can be learned using action learning?', *Organizations and People*, **3** (4), pp. 18–21.

Bourner, T. and Frost, P. (1996), 'Experiencing action learning', *Journal of Workplace Learning*, **8** (6), pp. 11–18.

Bourner, T. and Weinstein, K. (1996), 'Just another talking shop? Some of the pitfalls in action learning', *Journal of Workplace Learning*, **8** (6), pp. 54–65.

Bowerman, J. and Peters, J. (1999), 'Design an evaluation of an action learning program', *Journal of Workplace Learning*, **11** (4), pp. 131–9.

Brown, J. and Duguid, P. (1991), 'Organizational learning and communities of practice: towards a unified view of working, learning and organization', *Organizational Science*, **2** (1), pp. 40–57.

Bunning, R. (1997), 'A manufacturing organization action learning programme that has paid bottom-line profits', *Career Development International*, **2** (6), pp. 267–73.

Burgoyne, J., Pedler, M. and Boydell, T. (1994), *Towards the Learning Company: Concepts and Practices*, Maidenhead: McGraw-Hill.

Caie, B. (1987), 'Learning in style: reflections on an action learning MBA programme', *Journal of Management Development*, **6** (2), pp. 19–29.

Cannon, T. and Willis, M. (1983), 'The role and application of action learning to management development in the small firm', *Management Education and Development*, **14** (2).

Carson, L. (1997), 'Action learning teams: building bridges within a local council', *Journal of Workplace Learning*, **9** (5), pp. 148–52.

Casey, D. (1976), 'The emerging role of set adviser in action learning programmes', *Journal of European Industrial Training*, **5** (3), pp. 155–66.

Casey, D. (1991), 'The role of the set adviser', in M. Pedler (ed.), *Action Learning in Practice*, 2nd edn, Aldershot: Gower Publishing.

Casey, D. (1993), *Managing Learning In Organizations*, Buckingham: Open University Press.

Casey, D. and Pearce, D. (eds) (1977), *More than Management Development: Action Learning at GEC*, Aldershot: Gower Publishing.

Casey, D., Roberts, P. and Salaman, G. (1992), 'Facilitating learning in small groups', *Leadership and Organization Development*, **13** (4).

Chan, K. (1994), 'Learning for total quality: an action learning approach', *The Learning Organization*, **1** (1), pp. 17–22.

Chesterton, G. (1981), 'The Point of a Pin', in *The Penguin Complete Father Brown*, London: Penguin.

Claxton, G. (1997), *Hare Brain, Tortoise Mind: Why Intelligence Increases More When You Think Less*, London: Fourth Estate.

Coates, J. (1986), 'An action learning approach to performance review and development: a case history from the London Borough of Bromley', *Industrial and Commercial Training*, **18** (4).

Codori, C. (1989), 'Three experiences in action learning: audit training meets the real world', *Management Audit Journal*, **4** (3).

Cusins, P. (1996), 'Action learning revisited', *Journal of Workplace Learning*, **8** (6), pp. 19–26.

Dilworth, R. (1996), 'Action learning: bridging academic and workplace domains', *Employee Counselling Today*, **8** (6), pp. 48–56.

Dixon, N (1990), 'Action learning, action science and learning new skills', *Industrial and Commercial Training*, **2** (4), pp. 10–16.

Dixon, N. (1994), *The Organizational Learning Cycle*, Maidenhead: McGraw-Hill.

Dixon, N. (1998), 'Action learning: more than just a task force', *Performance Improvement Quarterly*, **11** (1), pp. 45–8.

Donaghue, C. (1992), 'Towards a model of set adviser effectiveness', *Journal of European Industrial Training*, **16** (1), pp. 20–26.

Dotlich, D. and Noel, J. (1998), *Action Learning: How the World's Top Companies Are Re-creating their Leaders and Themselves*, San Francisco: Jossey-Bass.

Dylan, B. (2001), 'Sugar Baby', *Love and Theft*, Sony.

Eliot, T.S. (1963), 'The Four Quartets', in *Collected Poems: 1909–62*, London: Faber & Faber.

Enderby, J. and Phelan, D. (1994), 'Action learning groups as the foundation for cultural change', *The Quality Magazine*, **3** (1), pp. 42–9.

Eraut, M. (1994), *Developing Professional Knowledge And Competence*, London: Falmer Press.

Ferguson, M. (1980), *The Aquarian Conspiracy*, Los Angeles, CA: J.P. Tarcher.

Finke, R. (1995), 'Creative realism', in S. Smith, T. Ward and R. Finke (eds), *The Creative Cognition Approach*, Cambridge, MA: Massachusetts Institute of Technology.

Forrester, A. and Webb, S. (1992), 'Action learning in action', in *Working and Learning Together: Development as a Strategic Activity: Papers From 2nd Public Service Conference*, London: Association for Management Education and Development.

Foy, N. (1977), 'Action learning comes to industry', *Harvard Business Review*, **55** (5).

Frank, H. (1996a), 'Will the future of management development involve action learning?', *Education and Training*, **33** (8), pp. 4–9.

Frank, H. (1996b), 'The use of action learning in British higher education', *Education and Training*, **38** (8), pp. 7–15.

French, W. and Bell, C. (1999), *Organization Development: Behavioral Science Interventions for Organization Improvement*, Englewood Cliffs, NJ: Prentice-Hall.

Froiland, P. (1994), 'Action learning: taming problems in real time', *Training* (USA), January.

Galbraith, J.K. (1992), *The Culture of Contentment*, London: Penguin.

Garratt, B. (1987), *The Learning Organization*, London: Fontana-Collins.

Gaunt, R. and Kendall, R. (1985), *Action Learning: A Short Manual for Set Members*, London: Greater London Employment Secretariat.

Gibbs, G. (1988), *Learning By Doing: A Guide To Teaching and Learning Methods*, Oxford: Further Education Unit, Oxford Polytechnic.

Greive, I. (1994), 'Inland Revenue: making the change challenge', *Industrial and Commercial Training*, **26** (4), pp. 11–14.

Hale, R., Margerison, C. and Turner, C. (2001), 'Action learning meets e-learning: a European case study', *Training Journal*, August, pp. 18–20.

Harries, J. (1991), 'Developing the set adviser', in M. Pedler (ed.), *Action Learning In Practice*, 2nd edn, Aldershot: Gower Publishing.

Harrison, R. (1996), 'Action learning: route or barrier to the learning organization?', *Employee Counselling Today*, **8** (6), pp. 29–41.

Havergal, M. and Edmonstone, J. (1999), *The Facilitator's Toolkit*, Aldershot: Gower Publishing.

Hawkins, P. and McLean, A. (1990), *Action Learning: A Short Guidebook*, Bath: Bath Associates.

Henry, J. (2001), *Creativity and Perception in Management*, London; Sage Publications.

Hiscock, L. (1983), 'An action learning programme for between-jobs managers', *Journal of European Industrial Training*, **7** (4).

Honey, P. and Mumford, A. (1995), *Using your Learning Styles*, 2nd edn, Maidenhead: Honey.

Howell, F. (1994), 'Action learning and action research in management education and development: a case study', *The Learning Organization*, **1** (2), pp. 15–22.

Inglis, S. (1994), *Making the Most of Action Learning*, Aldershot: Gower Publishing.

Iyer, R. (2000), *The Moral and Political Thought of Mahatma Gandhi*, Oxford: Oxford University Press.

Jacques, E. (1955), 'Social systems as a defence against persecutory and depressive anxiety', in M. Klein, P. Heimann and R. Money-Kyrle (eds), *New Directions in Psychoanalysis*, London: Tavistock Publications.

Johnson, C. (1998), 'The essential principles of action learning', *Journal of Workplace Learning*, **10** (6/7), pp. 296–300.

Jones, H. (1992), 'Biography in management and organization development', in S. Mann and M. Pedler (eds), *Management Education and Development: Special Issue: Biography In Management and Organization Development*, **23** (3), pp. 199–206.

Jones, M. (1990), 'Action learning as a new idea', *Journal of Management Development*, **9** (5), pp. 29–34.

Kable, J. (1989), 'Management development through action learning', *Journal of Management Development*, **8** (2), pp. 77–80.

Katzenbach, J. and Smith, D. (1998), *The Wisdom of Teams: Creating the High-Performance Organization*, Maidenhead: McGraw-Hill.

Keller, H. *The Story of My Life*.

Keys, L. (1994), 'Action learning: executive development of choice for the 1990s', *Journal of Management Development*, **13** (8), pp. 50–56.

Knasel, E., Meed, J. and Rossetti, A. (2000), *Learn for your Life: A Blueprint for Continuous Learning*, Harlow: Financial Times/Prentice-Hall.

Kolb, D. (1984), *Experiential Learning: Experience as the Source of Learning and Development*, Englewood Cliffs, NJ: Prentice-Hall.

Koo, L. (1999), 'Learning action learning', *Journal of Workplace Learning*, **11** (3), pp. 89–94.

Korey, G. and Bogorya, Y. (1985), 'The managerial action learning concept: theory and application', *Management Decision*, **23** (2), pp. 3–11.

Laing, R. (1965), *Self and Others*, London: Tavistock Publications.

Lawlor, A. (1991), 'The components of action learning', in M. Pedler (ed.), *Action Learning in Practice*, 2nd edn, Aldershot: Gower Publishing.

Lewis, A. and Marsh, W. (1987), 'Action learning: the development of field managers in The Prudential Assurance Company', *Journal of Management Development*, **6** (2), pp. 45–56.

Limerick, D., Passfield, R. and Cunnington, B. (1994), 'Transformational change: towards an action learning organization', *The Learning Organization*, **1** (2), pp. 29–40.

Linklater, J. and Kellner, K. (2000), 'Anxiety and action learning', *Organizations and People*, **7** (4), pp. 11–18.

Logan, A. and Stuart, R. (1987), 'Action-based learning: are activity and experience the same?', *Industrial and Commercial Training*, March/April.

Lustig, P. (1995), 'What is action learning?', *Organizations and People*, **2** (2), pp. 25–6.

Margerison, C. (1978), 'Action research and action learning', *Journal of European Industrial Training*, **2** (6).

Margerison, C. (1988), 'Action learning and excellence in management development', *Journal of Management Development*, **7** (5), pp. 43–53.

Margerison, C. (2000), Editorial, *Training Journal*, November, p. 12.

Marquardt, M. (1998), 'Using action learning with multicultural groups', *Performance Improvement Quarterly*, **11** (1), pp. 113–28.

Marsick, V. and O'Neil, J. (1999), 'The many faces of action learning', *Management Learning*, **30** (2), pp. 159–76.

McAdam, J. (1995), 'Joint action learning: a collective collaborative paradigm for the management of change in unionized organizations', *Journal of Managerial Psychology*, **10** (6), pp. 31–40.

McGill, I. and Beaty, L. (1992), *Action Learning: A Practitioner's Guide*, London: Kogan-Page.

McGill, I., Segal-Horn, S., Bourner, T. and Frost, P. (1990), 'Action learning: a vehicle for personal and group experiential learning', in S. Weil and I. McGill (eds), *Making Sense of Experiential Learning*, Milton Keynes: Open University Press/SRHE.

McLaughlin, H. and Thorpe, R. (1993), 'Action learning – a paradigm in emergence: the problems facing a challenge to traditional management education and development', *British Journal of Management*, **4** (1), pp. 19–27.

McLuhan, M. and Fiore, Q. (1989), *War and Peace in the Global Village*, New York: Simon and Schuster.

McNulty, N. (1979), 'Management development by action learning', *Training and Development Journal*, **22** (1).

Mead, M. (1990), 'From colleagues in adversity to the synergy of the set', *Industrial and Commercial Training*, **22** (1), pp. 19–24.

Meehan, M. and Jarvis, J. (1996), 'A refreshing angle on staff education: action learning at Britvic Soft Drinks', *People Management*, **2** (14), p. 38.

Menzies-Lyth, I. (1970), *The Functioning of Social Systems as a Defence Against Anxiety*, London: Free Association Books.

Mercer, J. (1990), 'Action learning: a student's perspective', *Industrial and Commercial Training*, **22** (2), pp. 3–8.

Morgan, G. (1986), *Images of Organization*, London: Sage.

Morgan, G. and Ramirez, R. (1984), 'Action learning: a holographic metaphor for guiding social change', *Human Relations*, **37** (1), pp. 1–28.

Mumford, A. (ed.) (1984), *Insights in Action Learning*, Buckingham: MCB University Press.

Mumford, A. (1991), 'Learning in action', *Personnel Management*, July, pp. 34–7.

Mumford, A. (1995), 'Managers developing others through action learning', *Industrial and Commercial Training*, **27** (2), pp. 19–27.

Mumford, A. (1996), 'Effective learners in action learning sets', *Employee Counselling Today*, **8** (6), pp. 5–12.

Neubauer, J. (1996), *Action Learning Guidebook*, London: King's Fund Management College, London.

Newton, R. and Wilkinson, M. (1995), 'When the talking is over: using action learning', *Health Manpower Management*, **21** (1), pp. 34–9.

O'Hara, S., Webber, T. and Reeve, S. (1996), 'Action learning in management education', *Education and Training*, **38** (8), pp. 16–21.

O'Neil, J. (1996), 'A study of the role of learning advisers in action learning', *Employee Counselling Today*, **8** (6), pp. 42–7.

Parkes, D. (1998), 'Action learning: business applications in North America', *Journal of Workplace Learning*, **10** (3), pp. 165–8.

Pedler, M. (1991a), 'Another look at set advising', in M. Pedler (ed.), *Action Learning in Practice*, 2nd edn, Aldershot: Gower Publishing.

Pedler, M. (ed.) (1991b), *Action Learning in Practice*, 2nd edn, Aldershot: Gower Publishing.

Pedler, M. (1996), *Action Learning for Managers*, London: Lemos & Crane.

Pedler, M. (1997), 'Interpreting action learning', in J. Burgoyne and M. Reynolds (eds), *Management Learning: Integrating Perspectives in Theory and Practice*, London: Sage.

Pedler, M. and Aspinwall, K. (1996), *Perfect plc?: The Purpose and Practice of Organizational Learning*, Maidenhead: McGraw-Hill.

Pedler, M. and Boutall, J. (1992), *Action Learning for Change: a Resource Book for Managers and Other Professionals*, Bristol: National Health Service Training Directorate.

Pedler, M. and Boydell, T. (1999), *Managing Yourself*, London: Lemos & Crane.

Pedler, M., Burgoyne, J. and Boydell, T. (1991), *The Learning Company: A Strategy for Sustainable Development*, Maidenhead: McGraw-Hill.

Peters, J. and Smith, P. (1996), 'Developing high-potential staff: an action learning approach', *Journal of Workplace Learning*, **8** (3), pp. 6–11.

Peters, J. and Smith, P. (1998a), 'Learn to ask the right questions', *Journal of Workplace Learning*, **10** (2), pp. 169–72.

Peters, J. and Smith, P. (1998b), 'Action learning and the leadership development challenge', *Journal of Workplace Learning*, **10** (6/7), pp. 284–91.

Prideaux, G. (1990), 'Making action learning more effective', *Training and Management Development Methods*, **16**.

Proust, M. (1996), *Remembrance of Things Past*, New York: Vintage Books.

Pun, A. (1990), 'Action learning for trainers' development', *Journal of European Industrial Training*, **14** (9).

Raelin, J. (1994), 'Whither management education?: professional education, action learning and beyond', *Management Learning*, **25** (2), pp. 301–17.

Raelin, J. (1997a), 'Individual and situational predictors of successful outcomes from action learning', *Journal of Management Education*, **21** (3), pp. 368–94.

Raelin, J. (1997b), 'Action learning and action science: are they different?', *Organizational Dynamics*, **26** (1), pp. 21–34.

Raelin, J. (1999), 'The design of the action project in work-based learning', *Human Resource Planning*, **22** (3), pp. 12–28.

Raelin, J. (2000), *Work-Based Learning: The New Frontier of Management Development*, Englewood Cliffs, NJ: Prentice-Hall.

Ramirez, R. (1983), 'Action learning: a strategic approach for organizations facing turbulent conditions', *Human Relations*, **36** (8).

Reid, M. (1994), 'Action learning: a set within a set', *Training and Management Development Methods*, **8**.

Revans, R. (1971), *Developing Effective Managers*, New York: Praeger.

Revans, R. (1982), *The Origins and Growth of Action Learning*, Bromley, Kent: Chartwell-Bratt.

Revans, R. (1998), *The ABC of Action Learning*, London: Lemos & Crane.

Rilke, R.M. *Duino Elegies*.

Rogers, A. (1996), *Teaching Adults*, Buckingham: Open University Press.

Rogers, C. (1961), *On Becoming a Person*, Boston, MA: Houghton-Mifflin.

Sankaran, S. (1997), 'Sets on the net', *Today's Manager*, November 1996–January 1997.

Segal-Horn, S., McGill, I., Bourner, T. and Frost, P. (1987), 'Non-facilitated action learning', *Management Education and Development*, **18** (4), pp. 277–86.

Senge, P. (1990), *The Fifth Discipline: The Art and Practice of the Learning Organization*, London: Century Business.

Shaw, G.B. (1965), *Man and Superman*, New York: Airmont Publishing.

Smith, D. (1978), 'Action learning', *Industrial and Commercial Training*, **10** (5).

Smith, D. (1983), 'Thoughts on action learning', *Industrial and Commercial Training*, **15** (1).

Smith, D.J. (1992), 'Company-based projects: using action learning to develop consultancy skills', *Journal of Management Development*, **11** (1).

Smith, P (1988), 'Second thoughts on action learning', *Journal of European Industrial Training*, **12** (6), pp. 28–31.

Smith, P (1997), 'Q'ing action learning: more on minding our Ps and Qs', *Management Decision*, **35** (5).

Smith, P. (1998), 'Action learning: praxiology of variants', *Industrial and Commercial Training*, **30** (7).

Smith, P. and Day, A. (2000), 'Strategic planning as action learning', *Organizations and People*, **7** (1), pp. 7–15.

Smith, P. and Peters, J. (1997), 'Action learning is worth a closer look', *Business Quarterly*, **62**, Autumn.

Sutton, D. (1989), 'Further thoughts on action learning', *Journal of European Industrial Training*, **12** (6), pp. 32–5.

Sutton, D. (1990), 'Action learning: in search of P', *Industrial and Commercial Training*, **22** (1).

Vince, R. and Martin, L. (1993), 'Inside action learning: an exploration of the psychology and politics of the action learning model', *Management Education and Development*, **24** (3), pp. 205–15.

Wallace, M. (1990), 'Can action learning live up to its reputation?', *Management Education and Development*, **21** (2), pp. 89–103.

Weiland, G. and Leigh, H. (eds) (1971), *Changing Hospitals*, London: Tavistock Publications.

Weinstein, K. (1997), 'Action learning: an afterthought', *Journal of Workplace Learning*, **9** (3), pp. 92–3.

Weinstein, K. (1998), *Action Learning: A Practical Guide*, 2nd edn, Aldershot: Gower Publishing.

Wills, G. (1983), 'Management development through action', *Journal of Management Development*, **2** (1).

Wills, G. and Oliver, C. (1996), 'Measuring the return on investment from management action learning', *Management Development Review*, **9** (1), pp. 17–21.

Wilson, V. (1999), 'Action learning: a "highbrow smash and grab" activity?', *Career Development International*, **4**, pp. 5–10.

Yui, L. and Saner, R. (1998), 'Use of action learning as a vehicle for capacity-building in China', *Performance Improvement Quarterly*, **11** (1), pp. 129–48.

Zuber-Skerritt, O. (1995), 'Developing a learning organization through management education by action learning', *The Learning Organization*, **2** (4), pp. 36–46.

Further information

The International Foundation for Action Learning (IFAL) was created in 1977 and is organized in chapters in the UK, USA and Canada. It offers a range of information and services related to action learning. The UK chapter can be contacted as follows:

Pam Wright
IFAL Administrator
Department of Management Learning
University of Lancaster
LANCASTER LA1 4YX
Telephone: 01524 812254
Email: p.wright@lancaster.ac.uk
The IFAL website is at www.ifal.org.uk

Index